THE
GIRONDIN

"*Girondin:* a native of, or deputy from, the
Department of the Gironde, France" (*Dictionary*)

By HILAIRE BELLOC

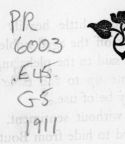

THOMAS NELSON AND SONS

LONDON, EDINBURGH, DUBLIN
LEEDS, AND NEW YORK

LEIPZIG: 35-37 Königstrasse.   PARIS: 61, rue des Saints-Pères

First published in 1911

TO

THE HORSES

PACTE AND BASILIQUE

NOW WITH THEIR FATHER JOVE

Οὐ μὲν γάρ τί που ἐστὶν ὀϊζυρώτερον ἀνδρὸς
Πάντων, ὅσσα τε γαῖαν ἐπιπνείει τε καὶ ἕρπει.

CONTENTS

CONTENTS

THE GIRONDIN.

CHAPTER I.

In which the Girondin finishes Dinner.

IN the year 1792 and in the month of August, in the early days of that month (to be accurate, upon the eighth), M. Boutroux, a wine merchant of some substance and of a singularly settled demeanour, sat at table in the town of Bordeaux, which was the seat of his extensive business.

The house in which the table was served was one of the old merchant houses overlooking the central quays of the city; the windows of the room where he sat at meat (without lights, for the hour was early and the summer sky still bright) looked up and down stream over some miles of the noble river which nourishes the town.

M. Boutroux sat at dinner. The table was of chestnut wood ; there was no cloth upon it : it was polished, and reflected good massive silver, the tints of early fruits, and the glistening of a decanter of dessert wine. At the end of the table his wife, a little, thin woman, erect and intensely prim, sat gingerly. The only other person seated there was his nephew, by name Georges, in age but twenty years, large in build, long in leg, dressed foppishly but rather negligently, and sitting in his carved chair, which faced the windows and the cool air of the river, more at ease and with less dignity than did his relatives.

He was not sullen, but he was bored, and the reason of his boredom was that M. Boutroux, his uncle, had for now more than twenty-five minutes very carefully detailed to him his lapses from right conduct, and the grievous burden that he had made himself to the household. His brown Gascon face with its crisped and curled black hair was half framed in his right hand as he leaned his head upon it, listening to the interminable harangue.

That speech had begun, as usual, with family history. The old gentleman had sighed over the unbusiness-like ways of the boy's dead father ;

he had discreetly deplored the poverty of Georges'
dead mother ; he had further deplored his own
childlessness—for Georges was now his only heir.
Next he had proceeded to his regular catalogue
of the various social ranks of the town, and
had introduced into that history, by way of refrain, a comparison between himself, the solid
merchant, and that very vile class of young
town nobility who, having next to nothing, and
never working, spent continually and were for
ever in debt—lacking probity and the proper
virtues for which the Boutroux had now since
the sixteenth century been renowned. He was
careful to mention several names which he knew
to be those of Georges' companions.

M. Boutroux the elder, stiff in a sky-blue
coat with silver buttons, gorgeous at the neck
with puffed lace, and a very handsome old man
under his plain white tie-wig (which he thought
the proper and dignified head-dress of a *roturier*),
was willing to admit that the extravagances of
his nephew had not yet bitten into the capital
of the family fortune. Had he thought it useful
to tell the truth (and Georges well knew it)
it had not bitten into a month of the family
income nor into a week of it. But M. Boutroux
the elder thought it necessary to enlarge. It

had of late become something of an amusement with him, and the indifference of his nephew to these remonstrances—an indifference only diversified by occasional respectful epigrams—exasperated him.

When he had done with the debts he turned to a more serious matter, and with a change of tone informed his heir that the shocking alliance which he had heard of from others must be at once and finally dismissed from his mind; to which decisive sentence, uttered now perhaps for the fifteenth time upon as many successive days, Madame Boutroux added a singularly decisive assent.

"I require you, Georges," said his uncle in the tone of a judge delivering sentence, "to put the matter wholly out of your thoughts."

"I have never entertained it," said Georges, gazing out before him upon the shipping at the quays, and replying as he had already replied as often as his uncle had thus spoken.

"If you have entertained it," said M. Boutroux, senior, "dismiss it for ever from your mind."

"It has been entertained," said Georges, as wearily as youth would permit him to speak, "to my certain knowledge by the young lady's mother and brother and by her sister who keeps the little coffee-stall near the bridge. I have lately learned that her confessor entertains it also; and from what I can make out, my dear uncle, you entertain it more fixedly than any of them. Though why you should do so, since it is not to your advantage but to theirs, I cannot for a moment conceive."

"Georges," said his aunt, "you are lacking in respect to your uncle."

"Yes, dear aunt," said Georges, "but still more do I lack respect and even tolerance for the sister who keeps the coffee-stall by the bridge, the mother, the brother, and the confessor—against whom I have a very special grievance."

"You must not reply thus to your aunt," said M. Boutroux with severity.

"I would not, my uncle," said Georges in a submissive tone, "had I not already so replied to the brother, to the sister who keeps the coffee-stall by the bridge, and more particularly to that very odious man the confessor, whom I verily believe to be in expectation of a commission upon the settlements."

"These are not the times, Georges," said his aunt, "in which to ridicule the priesthood."

"I admit," said Georges penitently, "that it was not very chivalrous of me, since the poor man has now for some weeks been hiding in a cellar which is the property of the mother; but you must set against this my considerable courage in speaking so frankly against the mother, who is no better than she should be, the young lady who keeps the coffee-stall, who is no better than she can be, and above all the brother, who I am very sorry to say is a patriot."

"We do not want you, Georges," said his uncle, "to introduce politics into what is a purely family matter."

"No," said Georges, "nor need they be introduced if we can only keep the brother out of it. A more ardent politician I never met!"

After this reply there was a short silence. Georges occupied it in watching a large pilot cutter set out down the tide for the bar under the evening light. He was amused to see the halyard block jam as they put her down stream, and he remarked to himself half aloud, so that his uncle might hear it, that from the way the people on board were handling the sails they appeared to be patriots also.

"You will not," said old Monsieur Boutroux sternly, "divert my attention from this matter by your jests. Where is the unfortunate girl?"

"Alas!" said Georges with a sigh, "it is my

perpetual concern that I do not know. From the gaiety and attractions of the place, Libourne has often occurred to me as being the probable sanctuary of her refuge ; or possibly Barsac, for, young as she was, she was always a little too fond of wine."

"You do not know her direction ?" asked his aunt a little suspiciously.

"Not for the moment, dear aunt," answered Georges with respect, cutting an apple upon his plate into four quarters, and leaning over it thoughtfully as though the task engrossed him. "Not for the moment. . . . But, oddly enough, she knows mine. I could wish that our responsibilities were more equally divided."

Having said this he pursed his lips, compressed them, firmly enclosed the four quarters of the apple in the pressure of his left hand, and with a silver knife of nice workmanship, the handle of which terminated in a delicately chiselled faun's head, he cut the apple transversely and let the eight parts fall upon his plate. At these he gazed with open and rather sad eyes as upon a ruined world.

His uncle could bear no more. Whatever entertainment he received from these daily excursions, he would not tolerate further impertinence.

"You will find," he said a little grimly, rising up stiffly from his chair and pushing it back from him, while the family etiquette demanded that his wife and nephew should rise at the same time, "that this flippant habit of yours will ruin you with men less indulgent than myself."

He took the napkin from his neck, folded it carefully, and watched his nephew do the same, while Madame Boutroux made the sign of the cross discreetly upon her black silk bodice, and having done so, smoothed her thin black hair from her forehead upon either side of the parting thereof. Georges was silent. He made for the door.

"Are you going out again, Georges?" said his uncle threateningly.

"My dear uncle," said Georges, looking at the ground, "yes. I am determined to settle matters once for all with the young lady of the coffee-stall, though I confess I dare not meet her mother nor the clerical gentleman whom she harbours in the cellar, which is the property of the family."

"You know that our friends from Laborde come this evening?" said his aunt.

As she spoke there came up from the darkening quays outside a sound of many feet hurrying, an increasing sound, as though a gathering throng had business further on beside the river.

The foreign war, the prospect of invasion in the distant north, the imminence of some vague but enormous trouble in Paris—these and the rising fever of the Revolution during the past three years entered the minds of all three as that sound reached them, and as the young man stood with his hand upon the door and his aunt and uncle watching him.

The old man called to mind his nephew's connection with the local Jacobins. He had heard in a confused way that some disreputable fellow in connection with that trull—her brother was it?—spoke too often at their club . . . he felt rather than knew that the noise of the Revolution was not only songs and visions but must have food to feed it, and that the rich would furnish the food. He was liberal—he trusted he was liberal. He had no superstitions, he hoped; he was for the nation. He was not an old-fashioned fool : not he ! He was for the King—if the King did his duty; but he remembered carefully (and had remembered for three years) that he was of the Third Estate. In his mind, which was so clear for business and so confused where passions had to be judged, he mixed up the impoverished young nobles, the bawling young lawyers with their scum of a following at the Jacobin Club, Georges' low amour—and Georges' going out that night. This last was nearest him. On that at least he could decide; and he believed it connected with all three—anarchy, the nasty acquaintance, and spendthrift youth.

"Georges," he said, "if you go out to-night you will never see me again."

"Yet if I do not go, my dear uncle," said Georges with due deference, "you will have the advantage of my society for but a very short time longer. Events will separate us into various prisons; for the brother of whom I spoke—her brother, my dear uncle—has certain designs."

Madame Boutroux gave a terrified look at her husband, but he refused to meet her eyes.

"In these times," said the old man, his voice rising, "threats of that sort are common. Men use," he continued still louder, "young men especially, the disasters of the State for their own purposes. I forbid you to go."

"Madame," said Georges, turning to Madame Boutroux, and thus addressing her by a term unusually solemn and not common in French families of his rank, "I do assure you that the

Club meets to-night, . . . so far as I know, the young lady of the coffee-stall upon whom I was jesting just now is not admitted, . . . she has not suffered the Illumination of the Seventh House, . . . she has presumably no acquaintance with the Sacred Triangle, the two Pillars, or the Thirty-third Degree, yet *her brother* intends to be present. Madame, he will suggest certain action against this house; he has heard that you have friends to-night."

"What are my few friends or my party to him?" interrupted poor Madame Boutroux.

"Madame," continued Georges quietly, "these people have the oddest ideas about comfortable houses. He will bring others against this house to-night; and it is my business," he continued firmly and rather sadly, "to interrupt him." He still held the handle of the door and gazed at the ground. "I propose to do it by persuasion; but if that fails, then in company with two friends, and with my little sword."

M. Boutroux, senior, was so incensed by the speech thus addressed to his wife rather than to himself—for his tall, straight nephew had turned his back upon him to speak to his wife—that his last answer was in a tone of constrained passion.

"Georges," he said, when the young man had done, "if you go out you go under my curse; and if you return you will not be re-admitted."

Georges weighed the matter, and made irre-solutely as though to sit down again.

"Let him go," said Madame Boutroux, quite white, for she feared the Jacobins.

M. Boutroux, senior, did not answer, and Georges, without turning to meet his uncle's eye, slipped out of the room, down the broad stone staircase with its gilded balustrade, and when he came to the porter's lodge at the basement asked that the wicket in the big carved oaken doors which gave on to the street might be slipped open for him. Old Nicholas, the porter, who had held him on the day of his birth, smiled at him indulgently.

"O Master Georges, must you be out again along the quays on such an evening as this? The whole place is in a fume! It is no time for amusement!"

"I'm not going to amuse myself, Nicholas," said the young man quizzically. "At least I'm only going to amuse myself by interrupting the amusements of others. Good Nicholas, I'll be back, I hope, within two hours."

Nicholas hesitated a moment, waiting for some thundering interjection from the first floor—for the whole household of domestics knew of the quarrel between the uncle and the nephew—but none came. He pulled the latch, and the young man stepped out with his little toy dress-sword at his side, in the full finery of his wealth, walking high in his dark silk and his gold chain at the pocket and his shoe-buckles of silver ; he went as erect as though he were on some military errand.

The little wicket as it shut behind him seemed to make a louder echo than he cared to hear. He did what he had never done before on leaving that familiar door, he stepped out into the midst of the paved way where now in the quieted evening no traffic ran or passers hurried : he forgot the distant clamour of the crowd, and looked up at the front of the house. It was silent to him. He saw no face and no gesture from any domestic. His people were not watching at the panes.

He sighed gently to himself and turned to the right to reach the great and noble bridge that spanned the very broad Garonne and formed a sort of triumphal entry on to the crescent quays of the city. He noted that the air was cooler, and also that the big clouds of a storm that must have passed far up the valley were drifting eastward majestically across the last light in the sky towards the distant Dordogne and Libourne.

CHAPTER II.

In which the Girondin talks Politics.

AT this crisis in the Revolution the bridge that
crosses the Garonne had, on the city end of
it, two large poles set one on either side of the
way ; from these long tricoloured streamers depended. Passers-by had attached, in the manner
of votive offerings, coins, little handfuls of wheat,
and faded bouquets of flowers ; for the Republican
attempt—and the masses of the populace were
already Republican in feeling—was becoming a
religion, and was blossoming out in shrines.

Georges Boutroux gazed at the poles and their
offerings curiously and a little wearily. At the
foot of one, in the evening light, he saw a woman
wheeling up a gaudily painted stall upon which
were glasses and appliances for the making of
coffee and the serving of other drinks.

She was a young woman of the mountain sort,
from a hundred miles to the south, very bold and

careless in expression, with dishevelled, handsome hair; her eyes were as fixed, as purposeful, and as rapid as a sailor's. They were brown eyes, and Boutroux, remarking them as he approached more closely, remembered that her sister's were less intense and perhaps a trifle more generous. He saluted her in the gravest manner, and she treated him in return much as a bargainer in the market treats a man whom he could quarrel with but hopes before quarrelling to make a profit upon.

"If you are coming to ask me a question, M. Georges," she said, "I shall not answer it you." As she said this, however, she smiled in a forced but ready manner.

"That," said Georges Boutroux gravely, "will depend upon the question. I want to ask where I may find your brother."

"Oh, my *brother!*" said the mountain lady with something like humour in her fixed eyes, which were set far apart in her head, and were strong in aspect. "All the world knows where my *brother* will be to-night."

"Yes," said Georges gently, "and I shall be there too, but I want to know where I may first find him."

"Really, M. Georges," she said with the

mercantile laugh which hundreds heard every day as they came to the little barrow to drink at evening, "you seem now as you seemed before, more intent upon the conversation of his ladies than on finding him. If he were really angry with you," she added a little menacingly, "you would soon find out where he is." And as she said this her eyes glanced at a spot somewhat to his own right.

He turned sharply round and saw the young man whom he was seeking.

The lady's brother was a curious figure. In quieter times one would have said that he had dressed up for the occasion or was on his way to a pageant; but in moments of violent civil tumult and of foreign war, when the State is invaded, and the most intense of political passions are in peril of final defeat, much may be excused.

He wore his own hair, not because he had been born a pauper (for recent political advancement had given him several francs a day), but because it seemed to him Republican to do so. In his right hand he carried carelessly—as a man to-day carries a pair of gloves—a bright red worsted cap imported from England, and of the sort that was then worn in England by brewers' journeymen, but was used in Bordeaux at that moment for a cap of Liberty. Round his neck was hung, as one might hang a locket, a large leaden token upon a leathern string. This token was stamped in strong relief with a triangle, wherein was further stamped the figure of a seated woman. This figure represented Liberty, and it was holding in one hand an axe and in the other a sheaf of corn. His great cloth coat was open at the throat and showed some inches of his hairy chest; the cuffs of it were turned up as though he had but recently left work, though as a fact he had hardly worked with his hands in the whole of his young life, and had not even pretended to do so since the time of the last National Federation which he had attended the year before in Paris. He was browner than Georges, shorter, but quite as Gascon. His hair also was black, his eyes resolute and determined, and his carriage betrayed that exceptional and virile courage which we associate with the valley of the Gironde—a military race. He wore knee-breeches of common stuff; his calves and shins were, by a curious affectation, bare. Over his feet he had drawn a pair of military boots, and he was foolish enough to carry girt on to him, by way of parade, a great curved light cavalry sword, to which indeed he had a sort of right; for he was one of those irregular bodies of volunteers which the anarchic politics of the time tolerated and even sanctioned.

This personage—Henri Sorrel by name, or at least by baptism, but latterly Aristogeiton by democratic adoption, and yet more lately, by a change of judgment, Miltiades—looked at Georges Boutroux without anger but with considerable valour. He asked him what he wanted, calling him "Georges" and using the familiar *thou* of the French, in a manner which, only two years before, would have seemed to a young man of the wealthier classes of the city, coming from such a person, like a blow in the face.

Georges saluted with an excessive courtesy, and "thouing" in return, and giving his companion his Greek name with a sonorous accent, said that he wanted nothing more than to accompany him, and to speak with him, as they both walked towards the meeting of the Section—to the Club.

The plebeian was willing enough, and they went off. As they went, the sister at the coffee-stall called after them with the loud, harsh, and shrill cry that women of the people use. Miltiades looked over his shoulder towards her, but Georges at that moment pulled at his dirty sleeve, so that he turned round again and did not hear. She had wished to warn him.

"Miltiades," said Georges Boutroux gravely, "do you know I nearly called you Aristogeiton? It used to be your name."

"I changed it," said Miltiades nervously, and a little sullenly—they were many together in the body that had turned towards the Club, and he did not wish to be made ridiculous. "I changed it."

"But why?" said Boutroux innocently.

"Well, it began with," Aristo-Miltiades was answering, when Georges interrupted him with reserved sympathy. "Of course," he said; "I see."

As the two young men went through the streets towards the meeting-place, others and others again joined them, as disparate as could be.

A little shuffling old gentleman of the local nobility came up last of all; he never by any chance met Georges without linking an arm in his and borrowing a little silver—and so he did to-night.

Two big stevedores from the docks were with him, silly and good-natured, delighted (but a little shy) to be mixing with the wealthy. One of them dug the aged noble in the ribs and hurt him. A pale young Jew who sold books and had keen, rather furtive, and very rapidly moving eyes joined in; he was a man who really expected something of the new world, and something apocalyptical, unnatural, and to his own advantage. He was full of things lurid and dramatic, but he was not sure the war would not be dangerous. A broken lawyer on the make was there also, with a fixed face and a determination to become a master of men—a thing which in his thirty-two most unsuccessful years he had not yet become. A grave young officer of guns was with them too, proud and somewhat sullen. They were a group of nearly a hundred when they reached the hall.

At the door there was no password; for though they were all of the Brethren, the meeting was not secret. The Sections were duly constituted; this was a meeting of the Section, and any citizen might come in. Yet several chose to give a password, flauntingly enough, to a little haggard man that stood at the door, for all the world like a man taking tickets at an entertainment; and apparently the password that night was "The Human Race."

Boutroux, as he passed in, put his hand for a moment on the shoulder of the little haggard man, who looked scared as he did so, and said, "Is the password to-night 'The Human Race'?"

"Yes—there is no password—certainly," said the little man, startled out of all knowledge.

"I'm glad to hear it," said Boutroux. "I thought it might be 'equality' or 'brotherhood' or something of that sort. I get mixed." He looked the little haggard man deeply in the eyes. "The human race," he said, "and be damned to it. But bear it in mind. We both belong to it." And with that he went in.

Several of the group looked at him suspiciously, but he turned to the one who seemed the most intelligent (and also the most suspicious) and said, "Believe me, gentlemen; it is profoundly true." He went in and took his place on a rough bench beside the others.

The room was long, low, and narrow: it had served in turn for a small wine-market, for a dancing-hall, and for a place of public meeting. It had latterly been acquired by the city for the regular meeting of this Section. Five dirty oil lamps hung from the apex of its ridgeboard, above the gangway that separated the seats upon either side ; and they swung but little higher than a man's head. Some three hundred men were present, of whom perhaps half a dozen were a little drunk ; the rest were sober. Half of the audience were smoking tobacco in pipes, as was

the custom of the populace. One or two of the
wealthier people took snuff from time to time.
On the platform at the end six solemn men
were grouped: three in the careful dress of the
middle class, one military and singularly dishevelled, one a constitutional priest — a country
parish priest with a heavy, careless look—the last
a tall, fine fanatical figure whose glance and gesture
immediately arrested the eye, for they seemed to
carry the whole spirit of the Revolution.

This last one rose, struck the table with
a hammer, and asked for the minutes of the
last meeting. The old and decrepit noble at
Boutroux's side protested. It was a meeting of
the Section, he urged, not of the Jacobin Club.
He was there as a member of the Section, not
of the Club.

Grumblings began to arise ; several citizens cast
doubts upon the interrupter's private morals, while
one deep-voiced man in his immediate neighbourhood compared him successively to a number of
insignificant animals. Boutroux pulled the old
noble down sharply by the tail of his laced coat;
he tore it, and then, to apologise for an unworthy
action, whispered in his ear with something of the
license that is permitted to a creditor.

"I am here for something really important,

M. de Riserac. You will do me a favour by not angering them."

The old man's interruption was neglected. Every man there was of the Club, and the meeting soon proved itself not a gathering of the Section nor a debate between electors, but a strict meeting of that organisation which within two days was to raise Paris in arms, to storm the palace, and conquer the executive power throughout the whole country.

The minutes were read briefly, passed by a show of hands only interrupted by a drunken man who tried to speak and failed and was treated by the President to a short lecture on the civic virtue of sobriety. Then without speeches and without delay the bureau upon the platform proceeded to business, and the first item read was a list; it was a list of "men to respond to the call in case of necessity." Name after name was droned out, and approved. Nearly every name was known either by its attachment to the new revolutionary militia forces or the public rhetoric of the town, or by a recommendation from the mother society in Paris. The list was approved in its entirety, and every man present knew who could be depended upon when—for every man now knew that fighting was not far off—the people might be called upon to rise.

When that was over, speeches were made, simple and violent enough. They concluded with a short and very fine piece of measured prose which that presiding fanatic had prepared —and worthily prepared.

As he spoke the audience saw the invaders already upon the march, the treason of the King and of the Executive Government, the garrisoning of the palace, and the necessity for national action and for the destruction of all that impeded it. The careful, classical sentences suited the long tradition of those minds. The rhythm of those phrases sobered the drunkards : they filled the rest with that cold enthusiasm which, in the Latin tradition, is the precursor both of heroic deeds and of crimes.

The President's speech over, there succeeded short violent interjections rather than harangues, each raising the heat of the gathering in some degree until at last emotion was exhausted, and at a signal from the chair the evening ended.

Miltiades rose in his place. "I have urgent news before we separate," he cried, and he looked at Georges sideways, but Georges sat tight.

"Is it information for the Executive?" asked the President.

"Yes, information of a plot."

As Miltiades shouted the word, many stopped on their way out, and several turned as though to stay.

The President called to them all in his clear tones, "The sitting is over, citizens; there is no need for any to remain save the Executive. We shall do our duty."

At this they moved outward again, but slowly, towards the door.

It was about half-past nine o'clock. The room had emptied.

Boutroux put his hand a little heavily upon Miltiades' shoulder, shook off the aged noble who tried to cling to him, and said to the plebeian,—

"Miltiades, I will come up to the table with you and help you. I may be of use."

The plebeian was not without sentiment. He had always thought it hard to hide from Boutroux where his sister might for the moment be : he felt himself under a sort of obligation mixed, as it must always be with men of peasant blood, with the hope of future gain. Anyhow he felt awkward to have Boutroux there.

"It's secret," he muttered; "you can't help."

"Who knows?" replied Georges pensively; "a friend is always useful. For instance, you might be wrong and so get suspected. . . . I had better come."

They went up to the table together. The men on the platform were engaged upon another list in a smaller book; it was closed rapidly over the finger of the President as they approached.

"What have you to say, Citizen?" he asked solemnly of Miltiades, ignoring Georges altogether.

Miltiades mumbled a few words sullenly.

"We know the house," answered the President; "we have marked it."

Here Boutroux intervened.

"I ought to know against whom action may be taken," he said, "if action becomes necessary."

"Action will be necessary," said the President, speaking fixedly like a statue.

"Yes," answered Boutroux as easily as ever, "and we must all know against whom it will be taken, or there will be confusion." Then as though he were mentioning a taste in wine, he added, "I have several reasons for saying that I would much rather it were not taken, among other places, against my uncle's house. For instance, I live there."

The President, looking at him with a complete

sincerity, said, "If I call on you, Citizen, you must do your duty."

"Certainly, Citizen," said Boutroux ritually. (He had made young ladies laugh often enough at the absurd term "Citizen;" he had a killing trick of using it suddenly in drawing-rooms.)

"Citizen, no just man will suffer," the President intoned, "and the property of all, just or unjust, will be spared by the majesty of the People."

"That is it," said Boutroux gently, smiling at that member of the six directors who seemed to him the coarsest and most human. "I took the trouble of coming up here, before getting into the much fresher air outside, to tell you that my uncle is among the just, and that it will be singularly convenient to me if his property should be quite particularly secure in trusting to the majesty of the People."

Miltiades looked awkward for a moment, and Boutroux waited for his answer.

"No one threatens your uncle," said the fanatic President gravely, but he was imprudent enough to add, "Wealth is indifferent to the high indignation of the people; but if traitors. . . ."

"You have furnished me with the very word," interrupted Boutroux. "The very word! I had it on the tip of my tongue, and now you remind me of it! President, the whole point is, that my uncle does not happen to be a traitor; it is a most important point both to him and to the justly indignant populace. It is a major point; on such a night as this a really capital point," and Boutroux shot a glance at the coarse man in whom he hoped to find an ally.

The coarse man, who was also good-humoured and loose, burst into a loud guffaw. "Citizen!" said he, "Citizen! I verily believe you are a Gaul!"

The Curé, who had been to school thirty years before, took a pinch of snuff and said "Attic salt," twice, but no one understood him nor cared for what he said. The coarse man suddenly began to laugh and could not cease from laughing; he laughed until the tears came into his eyes. The fanatic was indignant, but the virility of the coarse man conquered.

"Citizen Boutroux," he coughed between his gasps, "you will be the death of me! Ho! you will be the death of me! I like you as much in a revolution as I did in the wine-cellars before revolutions were dreamed of, and when you were a silly lad of seventeen. Lord! boy, patriotism can go bail and give security like anything else!"

"Exactly," said Boutroux. "The shame and the disgrace that I should feel if my family should prove in any way lacking to the popular cause would make me forget a paltry loss of cash. Still, since we are speaking of cash"—he looked round him—"I am willing to call it a thousand. Will the Section accept such a guarantee? Shall I sign?"

"We are better without signatures," said the President calmly, "and there is no price for treason."

"Precisely," said Boutroux. "I wanted to add that at the first hint of treason—nay, of cooling enthusiasm—escheat the money. But there is something I should warn you against. My uncle sometimes suffers from delusions, and when he is not himself he talks at random. Would you only remember that on the guarantee of yet another thousand I guarantee him— if he say anything uncivic—to be suffering from delusions?"

"Do you warrant his words?" said the President, turning to Miltiades.

"I've given true information," grumbled the man. "I might have shown favour, and I did not." He wished that thousand had come his way; he suspected that if he held firm another sum might find its way to him.

"A thousand livres," said the President, falling into the old vocabulary and talking stiffly, "is but the wages of an honest labouring citizen for one year ; and to men like you," he added sternly to Boutroux, "it is but the price of a debauch—and Liberty is not to be bought, nor is the Nation. Nevertheless we will accept your guarantee."

"Especially about the delusions," said the fat man who kept the wine-cellar, laughing again uproariously.

"Yes," answered Boutroux quietly, "that is the point I most particularly wish to make. My uncle sometimes puts things in such an exasperating way!" And he sighed. "But I am guaranteeing in that amount that he means well. And here," said he, suddenly pulling out a bunch of dirty notes, "is half of it. And the other half," he said, sighing again as though he were intolerably bored, "on the day after you may have had occasion to visit him."

The President locked the money into a metal box, wherein he also put a minute of the name and time. Then they went out all in company.

Miltiades, walking beside Boutroux, looked at him now and again in the darkness with curiosity, with fear, and with some respect.

"I had to do my duty," he said. . . .

Boutroux did not answer, but strode on.

"I had to do my duty," said Miltiades again; there was swagger in his tone, and at the same time a hint of bargaining. "My sister . . ." he continued.

"There now," caught up Boutroux pleasantly, "that fatal topic. . . ! Do you know, Aristogeiton—Miltiades, I mean—if there is one subject on which my uncle and you might differ (should you do him the honour to visit him with the deputation) . . ."

"You are your own master, and it's all in your own hands," answered Miltiades savagely. "Your house and your uncle and all he has . . . you may keep it or lose it."

"Precisely," answered Georges.

CHAPTER III.

In which the Sovereign People play the Fool.

FOR the next few minutes they strode side by side in silence, the others at their heels.

The street upon that August night was oppressive with a heavier air than Boutroux had expected upon leaving that closed, packed, and heated lamp-lit hall. A complete stillness presaged thunder, and one could just see to the northward, above the broad river, high banks of cloud making a black emptiness against the few stars of the zenith.

They all went on together through another hundred yards of narrow ways, to where an old arch spanned a lane—on the way to the broad quays; there the little group would disperse, but on their way it was their business to cross through the courtyard of an inn which, in the labyrinth of the old town, the thoroughfare skirted from one arched house to another, and the courtyard

was a rectangle of uneven pavement lying to
one side of the kennel. As they came to this
through the tunnel of the arch, they heard voices
and movement in the recessed courtyard beyond :
they saw the glare of great lamps contrasting
with the tiny glimmer of the oil lantern which
the Corporation maintained slung above that open
way, and Boutroux heard Miltiades call over
his shoulder to his companions that it must be
the Paris courier with news.

Two or three score men, not more, of every
age and dress, were gathered in a little group
round the high carriage with its tarpaulin already
cast over it and its stack of unlowered luggage
strapped upon the roof. The shafts were leaning
upright and back against the body of the vehicle,
for the horses had been taken out of it. Up
on the box-seat, holding a carriage lamp close
to a printed sheet, stood one of the postilions
familiar to the little crowd under the name of
Arnan, and they encouraged him to read with
jests and occasional applause.

The head ostler came out in the midst of this
as the men from the Section joined the rest,
Boutroux and Miltiades with them ; he called to
the postilion angrily to come down, and received
for his pains a mixed volley from the crowd :

some asking him why he was not in Condé's army, some why he was not with the Prussians, some bidding him go and garrison the King's Palace in Paris. The man was old, grim-faced, and brave; he answered, as though he were a crowd himself instead of one man against so many, that rather than be a traitor to his King he would drown himself in the Gironde.

A large fat boy standing near him said: "Perhaps you will be saved the trouble." The ostler threw him to the ground. There was the beginning of a scuffle, when the high voice of the postilion, continuing to read, withdrew the rioters from the beginning of their riot, and the old ostler, muttering a native curse and signing the cross upon himself, went back into the darkness of his stables until it should please his subordinate to finish his patriotic work.

The postilion continued to read: "There were rumours; the invaders were upon the march; they had not crossed the frontier; La Fayette had certainly betrayed the State." . . . . At the mere name of La Fayette a dozen of them booed so loudly that the renewed assertion of that man's betrayal was lost in the noise. The postilion held up his hand and continued to read:—

"It is certain that the Executive power will

arm the Tuileries. His guard of foreign mercenaries has already received orders to march
from Rueil ; several of the Sections in Paris
have taken Austrian gold and have betrayed
the State and are marching to aid the King."

At this point in the postilion's reading a very
large foolish man, with a face inordinately red,
said thickly : "That is a lie !"

The postilion showed some pride of bearing.
"Gentlemen," he said, "the citizen is drunk !"

"That is quite true," said the citizen in question,
"and also you are a liar."

Two of his neighbours fell upon the interrupter
and began to hit him rather gently with their
fists, saying, "Hold your tongue, fool ; we want
to hear the news."

He was drunkenly gentle with them in turn,
but continued to mutter : "It is a lie ! All the
Sections are loyal to the Revolution." Then he
added a little inconsequently, "and the King
is a pig !" But he did not interrupt again.

The postilion continued his reading : "The
volunteers enlisted already number eleven thousand. The Federals from Marseilles rival in zeal
for Liberty the Federals from Bordeaux." . . .
This sentence he had made up, and it sounded
well. There were murmurs of approval. "It

is the general opinion," read on the postilion sententiously, "of those best informed in the capital, that events cannot be long delayed."

"You hear that?" said Miltiades, in a feverish whisper to Boutroux, as the postilion went on with his news.

"I do," said Boutroux gravely, smiling to himself in the darkness and watching calmly the mobile, uncontrolled face of the postilion as the light of the carriage lamp picked it out against the darkness. "It is very pregnant. Events! If that were all, it would be no great matter; but the devil of it is," he added thoughtfully and as though weighing his words, "the devil of it is they will not be long delayed."

All this while the crowd was increasing. Young lads had run from its outskirts to summon newcomers, until the throng had grown to be many hundreds strong, and filled up the whole of the courtyard, making a packed and rather ill-tempered mass in its darker corners. These late comers only heard the last words — they were a proclamation that the "country was in danger," and an appeal to the revolutionary party for volunteers.

The night with all, and wine with many, had led to exaltation, when—at that most ill-timed occasion—a great gilt coach, lumbering, drawn by four fat horses, the two near mounts ridden by postilions in antiquated livery, tried to force its way from the one arch to the other along the thoroughfare. The crowd was too dense for its passage, and a rumour rose about it. The rumour grew to a loud quarrel; a bare-armed blacksmith in his leathern apron tore at the hinged door until it gave way. A moment more and the two postilions were dragged from their saddles, there were cries, and after the cries blows.

The interest of the mob turned from the reader of the dispatch on the box-seat of the diligence to this new adventure. Some said it was the Mayor, others mentioned the name of an unpopular squire who had stuck out for the old wages in the vineyards. Others of simpler mind said that any one travelling in such a splendid coach must necessarily be an Austrian spy.

Meanwhile, within the coach, women's voices shrilly protested against the indignity and the danger; and Boutroux, edging through the crowd, observed (and sighed as he observed them) two friends of his aunt's, decayed gentry of Laborde, down river, whom she affected for their noble name. They must have come that moment from his uncle's house, and Georges smelt danger.

Round the coach one of those spontaneous committees which the Revolution had the genius to form at a moment's notice was already chosen ; its leader was naturally the man who had presided at the meeting of the Section from which they had all just come.

The two ladies were on foot at the step of their carriage, still protesting in a torrent of complaint : he was gravely putting questions in the manner of a judge, deciding what the proper action of The People should be, and he was re-iterating with quiet insistence,—

"We *must* know, ladies, otherwise how can we form a reasoned judgment ?"

Since they would not answer, but continually threatened and implored by turns, the evidence of one of the riders was taken ; and to the formal question whence they had come and whither they were going, this man answered that they had come from a social evening at the house of M. Boutroux, the merchant, and as for their destination, it was no further than the Hotel of the Shield, in that same city.

The President gravely told them that that was enough, and that it would have saved much

trouble had answers been given earlier. He
named two men who happened to be roughly
armed, one with a sort of crowbar, the other
with an old sword, and told them off to hold
the horses' bridles and to lead them to that hotel,
so that there should be no misunderstanding.

The coach thus escorted went off, pitifully
enough, the packed crowd pressing upon itself
with a sort of spontaneous discipline to make
way for the vehicle; the door of the carriage
with its dingy coat of arms, torn off its hinges,
lay smashed upon the ground; a man lifted a
painted portion of it and denounced the sign of
nobility; the old ladies re-entered their gaping
vehicle, and with such dignity as they could
command resumed their way.

When they had passed and the crowd had
closed again behind them, it was as Boutroux
feared: the President, stepping up on to the
three stones which served as a mount to the
inn, very gravely announced to the mob that
there had plainly been held—or was perhaps
still holding—a meeting at the house of Citizen
Boutroux, a man suspected by some and marked
for a deputation; that it was the duty of all
patriots to see whether the local Austrian Committee had not held one of its political meetings

there that night. He said he would not dwell
upon the armorials of the carriage, nor upon the
unusual hour of its appearance, nor upon the
insolence displayed by the occupants of it towards the people. He begged them, in their
approaching visit to the Boutroux town-house,
to respect the rights of a Citizen, but at the
same time to remember those of the State and
of the Revolution.

For five minutes more he indulged in the
rhetoric proper to the time, and when he got
down from his eminence the thousand or so
that had now gathered in that small space were
already marshalled for an attack. A woman of
the market-place who had stopped casually upon
her way home to see why so many had been
drawn together, thought it proper to strike up
the new hymn of the Marseilles men, which,
three weeks before, had reached the city. And
the whole company of them took in a lurching
way the shortest line for the quays and the
wealthy houses—and with them went Georges
Boutroux, cursing their betrayal, heartily wishing
his money back in his pocket, communing with
himself and deciding that the best plan in a critical
moment was to have no plan.

As he went, Miltiades, who still stuck close

to him, nudged him maliciously in the ribs and
said : "You will do your duty, Citizen ?"

"Certainly, Citizen," said Boutroux gravely.
"It is the only trade I know." He made it
his business, as they went through the narrow
paved lanes between the tall old houses, to edge
a little to the left on the outer side of the
throng. At last, just as the head of the noisy
procession debouched upon the quays, he got
his opportunity.

He lurched away from Miltiades' side into the
shadow of a small alley, swiftly ran down it,
doubled through a yet narrower courtyard that
ran at right angles, and continuing his pace and
knowing every inch of the surroundings, came
out by the broad riverside at the very corner of
his uncle's house. He stood near the door of it
and saw the company which he had just left
approach, swirling and singing, up the quays.
He stood where he hoped to be unnoticed, in the
corner of the heavy carven porch ; the lamp hung
from its gilded and delicate metal ornament above
his uncle's doorway, throwing a complete and
blinding shadow over the spot where he hid.
There was yet another coach standing ready at
the door : the last guests entering it were making
their profuse farewells and handing their vales to

the porter and his wife. The mob was approaching rapidly, and Boutroux dared not step out into the light to warn the household lest the first rank of the rioters should note his action and burst in. The great oaken doors were clapped to just in time, the postilions cracked their whips, the coach rattled off swiftly northward along the river. A few larrikins pursued it, barefooted, shouting insults, but there was nothing worse. The mass of the mob as it arrived swarmed round the lodge window and clamoured for the master of the house and for his remaining guests.

Georges still lay hid, and watched them. He knew his uncle's temper ; he knew also, what his uncle did not, the temper of these men ; and he knew that his moment had not yet come.

For some moments the confused noise of the crowd, the song from Marseilles which the heavy market woman continued singing too loudly, too high, and too flat (though many begged her to be silent), the disputes of several as to what should be done, were all at last quieted, and the President stepped out of the half circle of their front in a manner somewhat theatrical but not undignified ; he knocked heavily at the door.

Through a tiny iron grating, perhaps six inches square, which was worked in the wicket of that massive oak, Nicholas the porter asked what they wanted.

Georges Boutroux, hiding there round the corner of the porch, his nerves all at tension in the shadow, had an odd feeling of familiarity and of home ; he knew that voice so well ! He had known it every hour of his life up to this last hour, and to hear it under such a circumstance seemed so like the odd and inexplicable grotesque of a dream !

A man in the mob shouted out : "We want to get in ! "

The President, more courteously, and in a low tone, reassured the servant. "Believe me," he said, "no such uncivic act is intended." Then in his clear chiselled voice, which could be heard, and which he intended to be heard, by all the nearest of his followers, he added : "We desire to know in the name of The People who is in this house and what their business may be."

The porter said he would convey the gentleman's message to his master. He snapped the shutter behind the little grating, and for perhaps two minutes the mob amused itself by most uncivic threats to burn down the house, and by other less congruous proposals, half of which were directed against the personal appearance of

its master, and half against that exceedingly unpopular character, the King of France and of
Navarre. The intempestive market woman had
again begun her loud Marseillian song—and
(from the honour borne to her sex) no one of
the Sovereign People had yet clapped his hand
upon her mouth—when a hush fell even upon
her at the sound of windows opening, the grind-
ing of the iron fastening that held them, and the
sight of M. Boutroux the merchant, coming out
into the summer night and standing upon his own
balcony, looking down upon the angry crowd.

I should be doing M. Boutroux, senior, a
wrong were I to deny that he felt the dignity of
the situation : he was a single figure, the lights
were behind him, he was on a fine isolated
balcony ; the Sovereign People were below. He
had read of such situations.

The fine and nicely poised figure of the old
man, its careful black silk dress, the more particular for such an occasion of ceremony as that
which he had just concluded, his obvious courage,
and perhaps the secret pleasure he took in so
dramatic an occasion, moved his fellow country-
men below ; and a lad who threw a tomato at him
and missed, was for this act cuffed about the head
by his attendant father until he wept with pain

and mortification—but he should have known the value of the unities in all affairs of the stage.

M. Boutroux, senior, spoke.

"I desire first," said he in very clear and precise tones, which unpleasantly reminded some of the audience of the tones of a magistrate upon the bench—"I desire to know, first, who is your spokesman and under whose order you are acting."

Above the confused noise of many the President, who knew his place, at once replied, and was at once heard,—

"There is no time for a vote, Citizen Boutroux, and I speak for those present and for the Section."

M. Boutroux, senior, looked at them for a moment in the calm dignity of his sixty-eight years and without replying. "I take it," said he solidly, "you are the Section."

Upon which reply the political lady from the market once more began her interpretation of the Marseillaise; but this time the respect borne to her sex was of no avail, and an onion dealer put his hand over her mouth so that no sound came from it but a sort of low moaning, and after that two gasps.

"You are the Section," said M. Boutroux again,

as though upon reflection. "Then I must certainly reply to your constituted authority."

There was no irony in his tone, and, though his mouth was set, there was none apparent in his expression either. This last, indeed, they could but dimly discern, for the light that singled him out in that conspicuous position shone from the room within.

"May I first ask what the Section requires of me?"

"We wish to know," said the President, standing and looking upward in a manner that he felt to be a little undignified and somewhat at a strain, "who is meeting in your house to-night, and for what purpose?"

"The answer is simple enough," said M. Boutroux with grave courtesy, and in a loud voice that rang over all the crowd. "There are present in my house to-night, and at this moment, myself, my wife, my six domestics, my porter, and his wife."

"Others have been here," said the President, a little menacingly.

"You are quite right," answered M. Boutroux imperturbably, and still in the manner of the quiet orator; "there have been in numbers, if I recollect aright, seventeen. In quality, five families of the neighbourhood, my friends. We have drunk lemonade and eaten fruit, and we have listened to a little music."

"We shall require their names," said the President, conscious that this dialogue was becoming ridiculous.

"The names shall be furnished you at once," said M. Boutroux; "a list shall be given to my porter and shall be handed to you. Have you anything further to ask?"

The President was in a quandary. He had nothing further to ask, but the mob had something further to do. The President was a leader of democracies, and he managed the thing well. He stepped back a few paces so as not to crane his neck ridiculously, as he had been doing; he turned a little so that he seemed to be addressing the crowd as well as this most unpopular and wealthy man, and then said with due solemnity, but in a loud and vigorous tone,—

"When we have received your report, Citizen Boutroux, we shall take the document (I beg you to execute it upon stamped paper) back to the Section—which I may tell you sits permanently to-night after the news from Paris—and we shall there debate upon your evidence. I think we are agreed?" said the President to the

Sovereign People, some of whom made a shuffling noise with their feet, most of whom were silent, and one only of whom, the political lady, shouted a wild approbation, adding the epithet "Pig," addressed to whatever in her mind stood for those social forces which did not meet with her approval.

There was a silence as though the Sovereign People were ruminating upon the wisdom of the lady's judgment. Then the President continued, in a manner matter of fact and absolute,—

"We shall leave guards at your door, and to-morrow, at our convenience, we will summon you for further examination. We hope you will be agreeable."

"You are very good," said M. Boutroux, senior; "my action will depend upon the circumstances that may arise." Then raising his voice a little, he said: "Citizens of the Section and your Mr. President, I wish you a very good night." He stepped back briskly, turned the iron catch of the tall windows, pulled the curtain across them, and so signified that the political interview was at an end. A large stone came crashing through a pane, and Madame Boutroux within that room, paling with fear as she did with every emotion, jumped.

"It is nothing," said M. Boutroux, raising his hand in a majestic calm. "These things are inevitable in revolutions."

There was no further demonstration. Indeed, had Madame Boutroux known it, she would have been pleased to see that the boy who threw the stone was reproved for his lack of civic sense by the President on the quays without; though that boy was little to blame, for he was but thirteen years old, and loved to throw a stone.

The noise of their feet was heard tramping off down the quays towards the bridge. There came a rhythm into that tramp, and a deep, robust voice started a marching song.

M. Boutroux, senior, meanwhile rang a little copper bell upon the table, and one of his servants appeared. He ordered writing materials and sand, and began deliberately to make out his list of those who had been present that evening at his little party.

Madame Boutroux, with fixed, angry lips and folded hands, watched him, and would neither interfere nor help. Once when a name escaped him, he asked her for it. She told him with a thin majesty that she would have nothing to do with it, and went upstairs to pray at her little chair. She prayed for the saintly Madame Elisabeth, for the Queen and the Royal Family, for the Bishop and the Clergy, the Pope, the Altar and the Throne, and she found in her book a special prayer for Times of Tumult, which she was careful to recite both in the French and in the Latin, for it had a virtue of its own.

As for her husband, he sat up quite half an hour longer, adding to the list of names a careful annotation showing how each possessor of such a name was legally entitled to travel, had taken no part in any movement offensive to the Department, to the Sections, to the Municipality, to the Assembly, or to the Crown. And this was not difficult, for, of all his guests, one only had been a male under the age of forty, and he was a very simple young man engaged in the commerce of wine, and chiefly occupied in learning the English tongue.

When M. Boutroux had completed his list and his annotation thereupon, he wrote at the bottom a formal sentence of protest against the interruption of his evening, a claim upon certain constituted authorities against the Section, his adherence to the constituted power of the Section, and then he signed the whole, sloping uphill from left to right in a firm, delicate handwriting, " Boutroux," and added his civic qualifications, his academic degrees, and the rest. This done, he sanded the whole over carefully, folded it into a neat cachet, and went down himself to the echoing basement porch, where he found Nicholas the porter very much perturbed, but very sleepy.

"Give this," he said, "through the grating— do not open the wicket—to whoever remains outside for its reception. Then go to bed. And, Nicholas," he added severely, "admit no one at all. Above all, you shall not admit my unhappy nephew, who is the author of all our troubles."

His face sterner than it had yet been during the excitement of this passage, the old man turned, erect and almost vivacious, neglecting the good-night which for so many years he had invariably extended to his dependants, and went firmly up the stairs.

When he reached his room he did not undress. He saw the light in his wife's oratory: it filled him with contempt; he locked his door, lay down (dressed as he was in his gala clothes) upon his curtained bed, lit a candle, and set himself to pass the few hours of darkness, until the danger might be renewed, in reading his favourite story from Voltaire, which was "The Huron."

CHAPTER IV.

In which the Girondin fences too hard and too long.

MEANWHILE, in his dark corner, hidden outside the doors of the house, Georges Boutroux had listened to all that his uncle had said, and to all that the President had replied, and throughout the scene had remained so hidden.

He did not disclose himself when the President chose two men out of the thousand or so present to mount guard before those doors during the night, and he waited with crossed arms in his dark corner until the mob with its noise and its occasional cheering, and its songs and its growing rhythm and military tramp, had disappeared into the night.

When they were quite lost, and the sound of them no longer reached him, he strolled along the neighbouring houses, crossed the broad quay to the riverside, leant against the stone parapet there overhanging the water, and with his hands in his pockets watched the blank window panes.

He thought it must be midnight. He had heard a chime a few moments before ; but whether it were the half-hour or the three-quarters he could not recall. All the casements of the house were dark. There was not even a ray shining outward from the usual watch-lamp in the porter's room in the ground floor to the side of the door, so closely were the curtains pulled ; and, pacing up and down before those doors with the regularity of soldiers, two men full of the importance of their mission, occupied and irritated his mind. An oil lamp was swung across the broad street at this point ; its light was just sufficient to show their figures.

The night was very dark indeed and perfectly still. The thunder clouds that had been rising ever since he had left the hall with his companions of the Sections now occupied the greater part of the sky, and already far off up river one or two vague flashes had announced the approach of the storm.

Georges strolled across the large paved way, sauntered in his fine dress, with his little sword tilted at his side, and his tall figure taller in the darkness, till he came quite close to those two

sentinels whom the populace had set outside his
uncle's portal. He stood not ten feet off, watching
them for some moments ; they knew who he was,
and they therefore neither challenged him nor
noticed his presence. Their regular pacing back
and forth continued to exasperate his mood. He
had paid his money to the Section ; he had bought
off such insults ; he felt himself tricked and
betrayed.

Each of the sentinels was armed after the rough
fashion of the populace in the Sections : one with
a pike, the other with a large old-fashioned sword,
a curved, light cavalry sword ; and peering closer
Georges saw that this one was—of all men—
Miltiades !

Georges hailed him, but Miltiades did not
answer ; he maintained his solemn pacing to
and fro, and disdained all interruption.

There stood before the house, a few feet from
the door, a rounded post of stone, convenient for
a man to hoist himself up on if he were willing to
sit and dangle his feet at some inches from the
ground. Georges Boutroux scrambled up upon
it, sat there and fixed Miltiades with his eyes,
slowly swinging his glance, pendulum-like, as that
amateur sentry stolidly paced to the end of his
beat ; swinging it back again as Miltiades crossed

to the other end of the measure ; and so for half
a dozen times.

Georges again broke the silence. It was as
Miltiades was crossing him for the seventh time
that he asked him " at what hour he would be
relieved."

The Jacobin did not reply ; he continued his
pacing. Georges continued his taunt, raising and
lowering his voice as the other distanced and
neared.

" It was a mistake to give money down," he
said ; " wages are best paid to the unskilled
labourer after his work is done—one can trust
him better so. And, by the way, is it not an
error to trust common men with arms ? They
might misuse them—nay, they might wound
themselves. Miltiades, my great commander, I
have a mind to sleep in my bed to-night, and I
paid for the convenience, did I not ? . . . I seem to
remember it that I bespoke an expensive inn. . . .
I did not pay with the object that any foreman
might pick men from the gutter to play at soldiers
outside my window. . . . I have a whim about my
house, Miltiades—I have a point of honour in the
matter of my sleeping-places, Miltiades, as some
men have of other more human possessions—
I like it to be left alone at night. . . ."

Here the sentry was crossing just before him again, and Georges added in a tone that was soft and exceedingly provocative: "When are you relieved? Must I wait here to discover, or will you let me go indoors first?"

Miltiades answered for the first time.

"I have orders," said he shortly, not so much as looking round on his interlocutor—"I have orders to speak to no one. I am on sentry-go."

"Well," said Georges, yawning and stretching his arms, "there's the devil of it! If I knew at what hour you were to be relieved, I would go off and have a glass, and come back to speak when you were more at leisure, and perhaps to share your wages . . . (though it is true I have mounted no guard) . . . and then I might slip in— who knows?"

Miltiades said nothing, but continued his solemn pace. He was almost out of sight in the darkness and back again for the twentieth time before he was addressed again.

"Miltiades," said the tall young gentleman, "do you happen to have about you another sword?"

"No," said Miltiades shortly, and passed.

"That is awkward," said Georges, raising his

voice a little with every step by which the other removed. "That is awkward, because I am getting cold in spite of the warmth of the night . . . and I must take some exercise. I have heard it said," he continued in a monologue which he modulated for the other to hear as he approached and passed again—"I have heard it said that it is quite easy to fence with a rapier against a cavalry sword. . . . I've even seen it done ! "

The swart Miltiades was stubborn and continued his pacing, crossing once more before that stone pillar on which Georges sat.

"And I believe," continued Georges, a little more vivaciously, "that it can be done quite easily . . . it would be fun to try." He slipped down from the stone pillar to the ground.

Miltiades had turned again, when he saw Georges Boutroux, standing in his path, suddenly draw his rapier—the little toy rapier of his evening dress—and put himself upon his guard. Miltiades halted. "I have orders," he said plainly, "to cut any one down who tries to enter this house." He looked squarely into Georges' eyes as he had done earlier in the night ; it was evident that he liked playing at soldiers.

"That is what I want to test," said Georges. "When you cut down a man you cut in carte. If you thrust, it is another matter; but if you cut in carte I can parry."

"Don't be a fool!" answered Miltiades.

He began his pacing again and turned his back to Boutroux; he was thinking, as he moved away, what he should do if his adversary proved stubborn, when he felt in the fat of the left shoulder, just below the shoulder blade, a sharp sting such as a man may feel when a hot coal touches him or the flick of a whip. He turned round furiously. Georges Boutroux had pricked him with the rapier. He cut violently at him with a downward stroke, awkwardly enough, and his cavalry sword slipped and spent itself along the other's easy guard; he almost over-reached.

"I told you how it would be," said Georges. "I am determined to see whether it is true or not that a rapier can fence with a cavalry sword, for I have always heard that it can." He put up his left hand for a balance, threw himself into the posture his fencing school had taught him, and played with the point of the weapon as though he were seeking some other mark wherein to worry the bull.

Miltiades growled. "I can kill you," he said.

As he said it he clenched his left arm behind his back and put his cavalry sword up to the guard.

"That's just what I wanted to see," said Georges, in the tone of a man who is playing chess. "I don't believe you can. I have a mind to stick you in the gizzard, wherever that may be : it is an organ I have often heard of but never seen. Meanwhile, lest I should murder a brother-in-law before the wedding, or a claimant in blackmail before due payment, or anyhow a good companion though one a trifle importunate for cash, I beseech you to settle it with me here whether a rapier can or can not hold its own against a cavalry sword. If you only knew how often I have heard that issue discussed ! "

Miltiades was not ready at repartees ; he said suddenly : "I . . ." and lifted his blade.

"I, on the other hand . . ." said Boutroux, and he lunged suddenly. . . .

Miltiades parried : he was too strictly occupied to think of calling the other sentry to his aid ; he parried, and immediately after he had parried he thrust too low, and all his weight went after the heavy blade. Georges stepped to the right sharply, the cavalry sword just shaved his hip ; he pointed and lunged home. Georges felt his blade bend hard, and the cloth give and the flesh. Then the steel went suddenly in—too easily. Miltiades' big body seemed to stumble up against the handle of the rapier and to lean on it ; for a doubtful, suspended moment in the half darkness Georges Boutroux could just see a puzzled look in the fellow's eyes.

Then the cavalry sword swiped vaguely and angrily in the air, and caught Boutroux a great crack in the rib; but that sword did not pierce a wound. Boutroux withdrew his blade with a sharp gesture from the cloth and the flesh ; and the hilt pulled away from the other's body, Miltiades doubled forward like a man who would vomit. The cavalry sword fell from his hand, held to his wrist only by its leather thong. Then down he went, collapsing into a heap of clothes.

" I told you how it would be," said Georges to that heap of clothes which still moved a little— he said it sternly. " You ought to thrust with the sword. . . ."

But from Miltiades there was no answer, except the low noise of a man not in pain, but so weak from something that he could no more : after that there was no sound.

Georges breathed deeply and went upon one knee to look closely into the dead man's face. The other sentry came up at a run from his thirty yards away in the darkness.

"What have you done?" he cried. He was a blond, rather inept young man, frightened at the circumstance, and his tall pike shook in his hand.

"Don't argue," said Georges shortly. He slipped the leathern thong of the sword from Miltiades' wrist and over the dead man's still limp right hand. He strung it across his own right, grasped the sword, stood at his full height, and said : "I'm a little blown, my friend!"

"What has happened?" asked the young man with the pike again.

"It is an accident," said Georges, "a very deplorable accident. You see, I belong to this house . . . and . . . and he knew it."

The young man with the pike looked down at the heap of clothes from which no moan proceeded. He turned the fallen man's face up into the glimmer of the light of the lantern where it swung high above them, from its cord across the street. "Is he dead?" said the young man with the pike, scared and worried.

"I hope not," said Georges, "I sincerely hope not. . . . But I tell you I belong to this house, and I want to get in."

The young man with the pike turned sullen.

"You'll have to answer for this to-morrow!" he said angrily.

"No doubt," said Georges; "but meanwhile I want to get into my uncle's house."

He hoisted himself clumsily upon the stone pillar again, his dress rapier lying useless on the pavement, with a few marks of blood upon it still; and he faced that other adversary.

"To tell you the truth, Citizen," he said nervously, "I am full of prejudices, and the thundery weather or something else has heated my blood."

The man with the pike edged nearer to the door and set his weapon forward doggedly. "You have killed my companion," he said, "and you shall answer for it. But I have my orders."

"You are not certain that he is dead," said Georges gently, "and I should doubt it. A man does not die so easily . . . but I do fancy he is grievously the weaker for his wound . . . he must have lost blood, my friend, or in that swipe of his he would have broken a rib of mine. As it is, I have a terrible great stitch in my side. I don't know what it is," he added, swinging his feet against the stone pillar, "but there is something I can't stomach in seeing two men mounting guard before my own door—or for the matter of that, one man." He felt recovered, and his voice was easy and strong.

"I have my orders," said the young fellow with the pike again sullenly.

"Now the problem," continued Boutroux in the same tone, scratching his nose the while with the forefinger of his left hand, "the problem of the cavalry sword against the pike is quite another matter. . . . There you stand with your great pike, and you have a reach, I suppose" (and he put his head on one side thoughtfully), "of a good six feet from your body, counting to the tip of the unpleasant thing you hold . . . it is certainly awkward!"

He slid from the stone pillar, stood up, shook his legs into stiffness, clenched his left fist behind his back, and put the sword on guard.

"You would be wiser to go before there is trouble," said his opponent as methodically as he could.

"That," acquiesced Boutroux heartily, "is undoubtedly true ; but it applies to us both. It is always unwise to meddle with edged tools." And he tapped the head of the pike aggressively with the flat of the great sword.

The other lunged at him with his long,

clumsy weapon rather half-heartedly and as though by way of empty menace only; he was evidently doubtful in the use of arms. "Get out!" he said.

"No," said Boutroux, "that is against my inclinations. I want to get in. If you would but go home quietly like a sensible man, carrying your pike slantways across your shoulder (if you feel more grandly so), or balanced level (which I believe is the more orthodox drill), nay, if you would but drop it where it is (for it is a heavy thing to carry about) and walk away like a good fellow, what a mountain of trouble would be saved!"

"If you do not cease . . ." said the other, raising his voice.

"Hush," begged Boutroux soothingly, "hush! no shouting, I pray! My people are old folk, and they detest brawling at night outside their doors. Why, they have reproved me for no more than having myself seen home by one or two jovial companions! Come, there are only us two, and no one to see. Which is it to be? Will you cover yourself with glory and be hurt, or will you be off? For it is getting late, and only just now I felt the first drop of rain fall on me, and I fear there's going to be a storm."

The other did not move. A patter of rain, big, slow, and heavy, began to sound.

"If only," continued Boutroux, "you had a sword as I have, how simple it would be! We would waltz round and round each other in the prettiest fashion, and clash and parry and make all the music that butchers make when they sharpen their knives on their steels outside their shops. But that ugly great pike of yours is such an intolerable clumsy thing that I know not how to deal with it." He advanced towards the door in one sharp step, and as he did so, the other plunged the pike awkwardly against him, caught the cloth of his sword arm, the shirt beneath it, and the skin, and grazed the surface of the flesh.

Boutroux was hurt sharply, and intolerably vexed. He swore, not loudly. He cut once and thrust twice, edging round his opponent, then he closed well in ; but that irresolute man, finding his heavy pike in his way at close quarters, had dropped his weapon and was clawing out desperately with his hands as though he would hold the sword. The blunt sword did no work save strike and bruise. Boutroux, more angry as he pressed the man back, struck at his head. The man weakly put up one arm to guard it. Boutroux struck again ; and he felt, or thought he felt, the fore-arm break at the blow. But even as he felt it his own arm weakened—it was bleeding badly at the new surface wound in his arm—and that curious, acrid, sinking feeling which goes with the loss of blood pervaded him in the darkness. Still he pressed upon that other, striking away with his iron, too close and too cramped, and more and more weakly.

The irresolute, disarmed, and tall young sentry, beaten like a beefsteak for cooking, bewildered, dazed with bangs about the head, and vaguely imagining that war must be a damnable thing, broke suddenly away and ran.

Boutroux ran after—and was surprised to find how stumblingly and ill he ran. He fell prone in the first few yards ; and as he lay sprawling, and wondering why it was so difficult to rise, he heard the echoing and rapid scamper of his late opponent diminishing further and further off down the empty stoneway of the quays.

He lay on there stupidly, listening to the flying feet with a sort of pleasure, hearing the tiny *tap*, *tap*, *tap* grow less and less, but still just catching it. He knew, as his bewildered mind received pain, wet, and silence all at

once, that things were changing. The earth
seemed to be moving. He thought for a
moment that he was on a ship : he felt woefully
sick. He tried to vomit, and failed ; and during that confusion he was aware that a violent
rain was falling. With one doubtful, unfocussed
eye he could see the splashing of the drops in
the lamplight. Then, for he did not know
how long, his mind was filled with nothing but
the perpetual crashing of thunder. . . .

*   *   *   *   *   *

He emerged from such a stupor as a man
may emerge from an ill-conditioned and unhealthy
sleep. The rumbling of the thunder, now more
distant, was the sensation to which he first attended.
Then he noted that it was lighter, that it was
dawn. The storm had washed the streets and
the air ; the trees far off beyond the river stood
out quite still, and wonderfully sharp. His brain
cleared as he watched them, lying there upon
the pavement. He shivered, and found that it
was cold.

He tried to raise himself upon his right elbow,
and suffered so acute a spasm of pain as he
had not yet felt in his life ; and when he raised
his head he saw the cause of the extreme weak-
ness which had made him swoon.

All round his right hand, as it lay limp on the pavement, was a mass of dirty, rainwashed blood; it was from his wound. He looked at the blood curiously for a moment, tangled in the cut of the cloth; he had never been wounded before, and he did not like it.

He turned his head weakly. On the wall above him was a ring, an iron ring set in a staple, such as men tie the bridles of their horses to when they stop and call at a house; he could just reach it with his left hand. He did so, pulled himself up with an incredible effort, and staggered to his feet.

"I have read a good deal about fighting," he said to himself. "It is quite, quite different from what I had imagined from my reading."

He took his right forearm in his open left hand gently and tenderly as though it had been a baby. He dandled it a bit, and moved it until it was somewhat more easy.

Then he remembered what he had read about the danger of dirt in wounds.

He very methodically took out his toy-penknife, and with the tiny blade of it he cut off all the cloth that lay above the wound. Then with the same instrument he cut the shirt wrist off as well and flung it from him. He bethought him what to do for a bandage. He cut a long strip from the upper part of the shirt sleeve, he staggered across the quay to the riverside, dipped the stiffening wound in the water by way of washing it—and wondered as he did so whether the water were clean enough to satisfy a surgeon—then he wound his strip of linen round and round by way of bandage, and having so done, quenched an intolerable thirst which he suddenly felt, and quenched it most unwisely in the brackish water of the Garonne. But wise or no, the draught revived him.

He remembered what he had next to do, and he went feebly, haltingly, very unready but determined, towards his uncle's door on the far side of the street some hundred yards away.

Even in such a dire circumstance Boutroux could not neglect the beauty of that morning. It seemed as though the politics and the violence and the bloodshed of the night belonged to some nasty drunken play-acting which he had seen upon a stage and had followed a thought too vividly.

The beautiful sweep of the city, the long and lovely crescent of the quays, stood lonely and clean in the early light ; the air was quite lucid since the storm that had purged it, and every mast and yard, and the very details of the ropework upon the ships, showed like things deliberately drawn by some strong and decided hand.

He felt an odd peace ; he remembered how quarrels even between an old man and his heir belonged to the night. He felt how very different was every new morning from the fevers of its preceding darkness ; he even began a sort of little comedy with himself : how he would speak to his aunt and uncle of what he had done ; how they would welcome him—for they could not mistake his courage or his devotion to their roof and their door.

He came up to that door—he was careful not to note under the dawn the body of a dead man. He knocked at the door gently, then louder ; there was no answer.

He tapped at the porter's window gently again, and again louder. He saw the curtain drawn aside, and old Nicholas' head appearing, a dirty cotton nightcap on his poll, a frightened look in his eyes. Old Nicholas shook his head.

Georges Boutroux beckoned towards the wicket, and that faithful servant hobbled out to speak to him. Georges did not hear the familiar drawing of the bolt : all he heard was the unfastening of the little shutter behind the iron grating, and old Nicholas whispering to him,—

"Oh, Master Georges, I have orders!"

Weak as he was, the mood of the night was still strong upon Georges Boutroux wounded, and he said, in a voice which was less than his own, and sadly: "What! Have you also got orders? Every one seems to have orders! And you, Nicholas, what are your orders?"

"Oh, sir," said Nicholas in a frightened whisper, "I am to hold the door!"

"Why," said Georges in his weak voice, and with the sickness coming back upon him, "that was what *he* said," and he motioned back with his head to the heap of clothes which had been Miltiades.

The old porter caught a glimpse through the little iron grating and shuddered.

"Master Georges," he muttered in another voice, "we heard a scuffle, but oh, we never dreamt! Master Georges, I would give my life for you, I would indeed!"

"And damn it all," said Master Georges, mastering his sickness, "I pretty nearly did give it for you!"

"Master Georges, I know the master—I knew him before you were born. He will not let you in this day."

"Old Nicholas, if you do not let me in before

the city awakens, and these things are discovered, they will take me and kill me. Do you know that ? "

"Master Georges, I could not make him understand. Master Georges, he said, 'Whoever you let in, even if you let in some one who would parliament from the mob, do not let in my nephew ; for I will never see him again.' Master Georges, he said that you were a traitor and the cause of all his misfortunes."

"My uncle," said Georges Boutroux in a sudden voice and with a weakening gesture, "is too fond of generalisation. We must respect this frailty in the aged." His mind rapidly surveyed his lessening chances. "Nicholas," he said, "I have no money."

"Oh, Master Georges," said the old man, "all I have is yours."

"Why then," said Georges, smiling at him, "let me have it. You shall not in the long run be a loser."

"And, Master Georges," said the old porter eagerly, "you should have wine if you are to go into hiding, and a little bread."

"Bread I can buy later," said Georges, "but a crust will do me no harm—and some sausage. As for wine, one can never have enough of it,

for it makes blood ; and that, you see, my poor
Nicholas, I have been uncorking rather recklessly.
. . . Only, dear Nicholas, be quick ! " And even
as he spoke a company of workmen half a mile
away were gathering at one of the barges and
beginning to unload. " The moment they see
that," nodding with his head backwards towards
the body at which he would not look, " the dance
will begin. And I was never fond of dancing."

Old Nicholas hobbled the step to his room
with fond tears all over his face. He came back,
and through the lifted grating passed a bottle
of wine which the young man hid in his coat
pocket, the end of a loaf of bread, a hunk of
sausage, and a pathetic bunch of assignats worth
on their face value two hundred livres.

" If you'll put your hand through the grating,
Nicholas," said Georges, " I will kiss it."

" Oh, Master Georges, it is I who should
kiss your hand ! " said Nicholas.

" I will remember to give you an opportunity
of doing that," said Georges, " upon some later
occasion—but whatever you do, do not break
your orders. The passion for obeying orders
is very strong in Bordeaux just now, and the
reputation of the family must be maintained."

The old man put out a hand like wrinkled,

brown, and carven wood through the opening.
Boutroux held it and kissed it gently. He turned
his back upon the front of the house which was
the only home he had known, and went off, not
toward the bridge, where he feared the traffic
and recognition, but rapidly to the quayside.

The many boats that lay there he surveyed
critically, though with a drooping and a wearied
eye ; he saw one hitched by a looser knot than
the rest, and with his unwounded left hand and
arm unmoored it. He stepped in, and sculling
at the stern with that same whole left arm, his
wounded right arm supported in his fob, he
gained the further shore. Without turning to
see his city or his home again, Georges plunged
through the growing grass of the aftermath
towards the vineyards upon the low slopes half
a mile away.

In this way did Boutroux begin his adventures.

CHAPTER V.

In which several Lies are told in an Inn.

THERE was long grass—not the grass of the aftermath, but the wild, self-sown grass of centuries—in the empty flats just under the spring of the vineyard hills.

Boutroux lay in the depth of it, contented in spite of the throbbing of his wound. He drank a portion of his wine, and said to himself, "The best of wine will taste sour of a morning." And he wondered what vintage it was, knowing that old Nicholas would have given him the best; but he could not decide.

He ate his sausage and his bread. He ceased to care very much, as drowsiness came upon him, either for that through which he had passed, or for the memory of his home, or for whatever might lie before him. He yawned in comfort, looked drowsily with half-closed eyes at the city beyond the river and the tall masts.

The confused recollection of the night, with its violence and its quarrel and its bloodshed, fatigued him, and at last fatigued him pleasantly, so that he fell into a profound sleep.

When he woke from this it was already afternoon. The sun was still high, but its light was mellow, and Boutroux woke to feel a mixture of two things: the content that comes from a deep and satisfying slumber, and the angry inflammation of his arm.

Then he began to remember. The light told him that many hours had passed, and that it was late in the afternoon; and he clearly conceived what must be happening in the city beyond the broad stream upon that Thursday, the 9th of August.

He sat up in the grass and peered with close eyes at the very distant houses, as though he hoped over such a stretch of land and water to make out what was happening there. He thought how, long before this, that which had been Miltiades would have been discovered. The Section would have met; the Club was not slow to action; the city authorities would have had to take cognizance of the death; and the police would be moving, too.

He wondered what witnesses they had found;

where they would think that he had taken his flight; whether the boat would be missed — he had had the sense to cast it adrift. He only hoped it had gone far down the stream, and had not caught near by in the reeds of the river bank. He wondered whether the Section or the authorities had entered that house to take the depositions; whether old Nicholas would lie or be silent, or would blurt out the story of his escape. He could see his uncle, whom the city respected and feared for his wealth, sitting dignified at his table and answering with disdain whatever questions might be put to him, and repudiating him, Georges, and leaving him to his fate; he had no doubt of that. Then he began wondering where news would be sent, and by whom. One thing grew clearer and clearer to him as these appreciations of danger succeeded each other in his mind: he must get off northward by the by-paths. And he only wished he knew more of the countryside.

As he so planned his wound began to pain him again and to throb. He attempted to remove the bandage upon it. It had dried, and he found the pain of tearing it off excruciating. He set his teeth, pulled hard, and partly opened the wound again. He was interested as well as suffering: he thought it rather grand to have a wound. It was evident to him that he must get it bandaged by some one who understood such things, and he reflected a little grimly that he might understand them himself before he had ended his adventures, for wounds were becoming common, and times were worsening.

"I will wait," he murmured to himself, "until I come across some more of this civilian fighting, and nose out the doctor of it. But meanwhile, wounds make one look a trifle too partisan."

As he was so thinking and speaking to himself, he heard behind him the creaking of a country cart, drawn by two stout, slow oxen, their heads bent beneath a heavy yoke. He saw seated in the cart a very small, weazened old man, with thin, grey hair under an extremely dirty felt hat, shaven cheeks and chin, and little eyes as sharp and bright as augers.

The cart stopped, and its driver asked Boutroux, guessing by his fine dress that he must have a watch upon him, what was the time of day.

Boutroux had almost pulled out the little gold watch with his name engraved on it, when he thought better of the matter.

"I cannot tell you," he said, shaking his head.

" I have had a most unfortunate adventure, and my valuables have been taken from me." With that he sighed, and continued to nurse his wounded arm.

The old man looked at him keenly. "Where did this happen to you?" he said.

"On the river," said Boutroux readily. "My people are already many miles up-stream. We were passengers from Nantes. My father and his family were still aboard and the ship anchored in the stream, when I offered two fellows something to row me along in the early morning to see the city from the water. They set upon me, and in the struggle I was wounded, as you see. They stunned me, and put me ashore here upon the country side of the stream."

The old peasant continued to gaze at him. "Where does your father's ship lie?" he asked.

"It is not my father's ship," corrected Boutroux gently. "He is only a passenger upon it; and I think," he added doubtfully, shading his eyes from the declining sun with his left hand and gazing up-stream to see if there were anything there in the semblance of a vessel—"yes, I think that is her moored nearest to the bridge."

"What is her name?" said the peasant.

"The *Helene*," answered Boutroux briskly, "the *Helene* of Nantes—it is on her stern. If you are going that way you shall take me there, and I will see that you are rewarded."

The old peasant shook his head. "I'm not going to the city to-day," he said, "money or no money. There's been fighting. . . ." He looked doubtfully at the young man, and added, "I will take you for one livre, if you can promise me that sum, to the nearest village upon the highroad, and there you can fend for yourself."

Boutroux remembered his tale. "My valuables, as I told you, have been taken from me, but I am good for more than a few livres anywhere on the highroad," he said. "The master of the post-house will know me, for one."

The old peasant communed with himself and risked it, and Boutroux clambered up by his side.

The jolting of the cart over the rough vineyard way caused him no little pain in his swollen arm. He found the very slow progress of the vehicle and the silence of the old peasant, still gazing over his oxen's heads and uttering an occasional rustic cry to encourage them, exasperating. The ride was not six miles, but it consumed three hours, and it was already evening and the sun had set when they saw before them the low-tiled roofs of a village. Their strict alignment told Boutroux that they stood along the great highroad. It was dark by the time the ox-cart had paced its humble way to the old peasant's barn in the main street.

Boutroux stepped down in the half-light, and the little old man, fixing him steadily and by no means politely with his gaze, said,—

"What about that livre? What about that franc?"

"Old man," said Boutroux, "will you give me half an hour to find it in?"

"No," said the old man.

"Yet you will get it so and in no other way, for I know a man in this village."

"I will come with you," said the old man simply.

The necessity of hiding his name and progress, and yet the necessity of paying off so importunate a hanger-on, and the necessity of maintaining his first story of a robbery, between them troubled Boutroux not a little. An idea struck him.

"Will you let me find it if I promise you two?"

The peasant shook his head.

"Will you let me find it if I promise you one silver scutcheon?"

"No," said the peasant, "I must follow you and get my livre."

"Very well," said Boutroux triumphantly, "you shall learn now that all this was to test you. For I have the money upon me, as you shall see." And fishing out the assignat, he paid it in the other's palm, trusting to an argument which should cover his tracks.

But the old peasant did not budge. He looked carefully at the inscription in the light of a neighbouring window, stretched the paper, pocketed it, and said steadily,—

"Then what you told me was a lie?"

"It was," said Boutroux cheerfully.

"How did you come by your wound?" asked the old man.

"Father," replied Boutroux, with something threatening in his voice, "if you ask me how I came by my wound or catechise me further, or by so much as half an inch show that curiosity in my movements which I do not choose to gratify, I will indeed show you how I came by my wound, and that in such a manner as to give you what I gave the man who gave it me. Believe me, father, when I have argued the matter out with you so, you will understand it more thoroughly."

The little old man was silent. He said,—

"I believe you are a bad son; I believe you are a wastrel. This matter shall be looked into."

He went to his oxen's heads and began backing them into the barn, and Boutroux, not allowing himself to exaggerate his pace, though he would have given much to run off and be free from this chance enemy, sauntered up the great road which the village lined on either side; as he went he raged in his heart. It seemed as though every one were the enemy of the unfortunate, and so raging inwardly he went on till he came to the extreme end of the street and saw there the sign and lights and heard the noises of an inn.

"In an inn," he thought, "one may always find diversion and sometimes refuge. An innkeeper is an important man in such a place : he will be the postmaster as well, and if I make it worth his while he will protect me from any insolence."

With that in his mind Boutroux sauntered into the main room of the inn, lifted his hat—crumpled with the night's adventure and with his sleep in the grass—and called for a mug of wine.

He was seated in a dark corner, some feet away from the half-dozen or so who were gathered in

the room. He leant his head on his hand to shade
his face from the distant lamp. Soon the wine
was brought him by the postmaster himself, and
Boutroux, watching that man's not kindly face,
beneath the shadow of his hand, asked if there
were any news of the city.

"Oh yes, news of a sort," said the postmaster,
eyeing him and his torn, muddy finery, his tousled
head, and his tired face suspiciously, but at the
same time hoping to entertain a customer who,
however bedraggled by weather or accident, was
by his dress apparently wealthy. "There was
trouble last night . . . it's led to more to-day."

"What happened?" asked Boutroux, sick within
himself in his anxiety for the reply.

"I don't take sides," said the postmaster, hesitating; "I'm a public servant; I keep this inn,
and I trust I serve my customers faithfully. And
the King also."

At the word "King," several in the company
laughed. The postmaster reproved them.

"I know my duty," he said; and then he added
in a lower tone to Boutroux, "You mustn't mind
my questions; the authorities have sent a list of
them from the city; they're looking for a man
who's wanted; and I've had to get every one to
sign as a matter of form since the coach came in."

He was silent for a moment as he drew from his pocket a sheet of paper—a printed form half filled in with writing. He looked at it, and then closely at the young man again. "What is your name?" he asked.

"Marchand," answered Boutroux readily, "Marchand, Victor. I was coming from Saintes, where my father is Procurator. He sent me in our carriage to reach Bordeaux this evening, but we had a spill. I walked on here to get a relay, but I shan't go further to-night; I shall sleep here."

"Oh!" answered the postmaster; he was relieved that this suspicious guest should sleep at the inn; it gave him time to decide about something. Meanwhile he reached down a great book, opened it at a dirty page full of scrawls, and pushed it towards Georges. "Sign here," he said.

Georges, mastering the pain in his forearm, signed with his uncertain right hand, "Marchand, Victor." And the book was replaced.

"What was the trouble in the city?" he said quietly to the postmaster.

"I tell you I don't take sides," said that functionary again.

A short, good-natured, low-browed young fellow in a rough cotton shirt, with a dirty stuff jacket tied round his neck, his arms out of the sleeves, broke into a loud laugh.

"You are too squeamish," he said. "You were ready enough before the gentleman came in. Fact is," he went on, looking partly in envy and partly in jest and partly with a sort of spite at Boutroux's ruined smart clothes, "they've been un-nesting some aristo's in the city."

"When ?" said Boutroux gently.

"Last night," sneered the young man. . . . "And to-day, good work !"

"That's not honest business," broke in the postmaster hurriedly, "and I won't have politics in my house. There's been too much already !"

A wealthy-looking peasant, elderly and solid, contributed his view. "It is our business to get the murderer," he said.

"Of course," said the innkeeper nervously.

"Oh ! the Club'll see to that," said the young man who had spoken first. "It's their man was killed—the man who killed him was a spy—and the old devil who sent him was at the back of it."

"We've no proof of that," said the peasant judicially.

"Well," said the young man, "the 'authorities' you're so keen on may catch the assassin first ;

but I'll put my money on the Club—they're all over the country for him."

Two grooms who were present nodded in assent, and a gentleman in rather subdued clothing and with a worried face—a lawyer, one would say by his appearance—who was eating an omelette and drinking a glass of wine at a more distant table, looked up furtively.

The young man added: "And I hope they scrag the old devil too!"

One of the grooms spat on the ground to relieve the pipe which he was smoking, puffed at it twice, and said,—

"Old Boutroux, to hell!"

The other nodded again, and said: "Yes, and his wife."

"Do you know them?" said the young, low-browed man in the shirt, glancing suspiciously at Georges.

"Yes," said Georges frankly, "I do. I know them well. It was only quite a short time ago that I was in their house. I should be sorry if anything happened to them."

"Monsieur knows perfectly well," said the innkeeper and postmaster rapidly, "that these men who are speaking are worthless. Pay no attention to what they say, sir. They speak and

imagine horrors.   Monsieur Boutroux is a good
Patriot ; he has repudiated his nephew, sir.   It
was his nephew who did it . . . a spy, sir, a man
in pay of the Austrians."

"He killed an honest working man worth ten
of him," said the elderly peasant.

Boutroux smiled serenely at them all.

"Your opinions are various, gentlemen !" he
said.   "It seems," he added, turning to the
innkeeper, "that there's been a murder, and the
police want the murderer ?"

The innkeeper nodded.

"Aye !" broke in the young labourer savagely,
"but the Club want him now, and they'll get
him—he was one of their own—the dirty traitor !"

"He was a spy," repeated the groom.   "So
was his old devil of an aunt ; and she hid priests,
and he was a Jesuit himself !"

Again the innkeeper begged for peace.   "Don't
hear them, sir !" he said to Georges.   "They're
scum—ignorant scum !   At least I can answer
for it in the case of my two grooms.   As for that
third fellow," he said contemptuously, jerking his
thumb at the young workman in the shirt, "I can
tell you less, for he has only been a journeyman
with me now for a week.   We all respect
Monsieur Boutroux here—we are most concerned

for him in his affliction for the worthless heir."

"Go easy, master," said the young workman good-humouredly. "The gentleman wants to learn."

"Exactly," said Boutroux. "I have not been to Bordeaux since six weeks ago, and I should be sorry if anything had happened to my old friends."

"Oh, nothing has happened to them," said the groom, spitting again. "What ever does happen to the rich?"

"You might be more gracious to the gentleman," said the postmaster. "One would think he had done you an injury!"

The groom then added a little more civilly: "It's what they did to the People, that's what puts our backs up."

"But hang it all," said Boutroux with an easy laugh, "what did they do? What's it all about?"

"Only killed one honest man by treachery, and would have killed a dozen others," sneered the groom.

"Oh, nonsense," said Georges easily; "I know the Boutroux well. Why, the old gentleman and his wife don't go about killing people."

"Do not believe what they say, sir," said the postmaster for the third time, in an agony lest he should lose wealthy custom. "They are worthless hangers-on and corner boys, these loafers of mine; they repeat anything they hear."

"Well, there was a man dead anyhow," said the groom, leaning his face forward angrily and showing his teeth, "because I saw him."

"Yes," said his companion, "and I saw him too, and I saw *what he was killed with*."

The postmaster was again about to intervene, but Georges put up his hand.

"Pray, sir," he said, "let me hear the story out. It is of a natural interest to me. Madame Boutroux was one of my own aunt's few friends, and my own uncle has spoken most highly to me of M. Boutroux since I was quite a child. I think it true to say that my uncle thought M. Boutroux not only a good but a *great* man."

Said the groom: "It doesn't take long to tell. They live in the Section of the Great Bridge; the Section heard that they were in a conspiracy, and that the committee were meeting in their rooms only last night, and that arms were stacked in their cellars. They sent a deputation to see the old traitor; he refused to see them or to speak to them. Just as the deputation was leaving the door, he appeared on the balcony and shot at them, hitting a large number, including a woman, a Patriot. I have seen her myself, and she told me of it. When they had gone, one man was missed. In the morning they sent to fetch him, and found him lying dead outside the door. That is the news."

"Dear me!" said Georges, betraying an increasing interest. "So the man was shot?"

The groom nodded.

"No, he wasn't," said his companion; "he was stabbed."

"He was shot, I tell you," said the first man angrily.

"And I tell you," said the other equally positively, "that he was *stabbed*."

"And I tell you both," said the young artisan, "that you are fools : he was stuck with a rapier. I saw the wound, and so did many of the crowd."

"There was a crowd, then, when you left the city?" said Georges, indifferently.

"Aye," said the young workman, "it was about two hours ago when I left. There was a large crowd roaring round the house. Don't listen to what they say," he added, shaking his head over his shoulder towards the grooms. "They've got hold of this morning's nonsense.

I'm telling you what happened. It was a porter at the quays. His sister keeps a coffee-stall there, and he's got another sister dancing at Libourne in the theatre there."

"I thought so," murmured Georges.

"You thought what?" asked the artisan sharply.

"Why, I thought," said Georges quickly, "it would be some poor fellow of the People who had suffered. It is always so."

"It is," said the young workman, to whom they were all now listening as the latest bearer of the most authentic news. "But it wasn't old Boutroux's own act, nor his wife's. Some in the Section went and apologised to them to-day at three o'clock, and they're going to give old Boutroux a civic crown. He's subscribed for the volunteers. He's all right. He's got a dirty dog of a nephew who used to go about with the Austrian party; got above himself—had himself called 'de' Boutroux; and then he would pretend to be hand and glove with the Section. Oh, he was rare! That's the man that killed the poor fellow. . . ." The workman pursed his lips and added the syllable, "Poz'!"

"Yes, that'll be him," said the grooms.

"I don't like to believe it; I knew the little cuss," said Georges. "He used to borrow money, and he drank a little, but I don't think he'd kill a man."

"That's the one," repeated the young workman, striking his hand on his knee conclusively; "that's him!"

The two grooms nodded. The postmaster said sententiously,—

"Well, one hears many different stories from different people, sir, doesn't one?"

"Yes," said Georges, as though he only half heard; he was thinking rapidly and hard—but as yet he had no plan.

The postmaster leant over to Georges and whispered: "The fact is, sir (since you know the family, I may as well tell you), it's the King's party who are hottest! They don't believe the young man did it—but they're down on him. They say he was a dirty fellow to join the Jacobins, seeing his birth and all, and they're keener on him than any! We've got one here, sir, in the town: an old colonel, retired—says he knows him. He won't let him go if he sees him!"

"No?" said Georges indifferently—and suddenly alive to a new peril.

But even as he said it the old man of the ox-cart came shuffling in and asked for wine.

The old man's glance was furtive. He touched his hair as ritual bade, and bowed, as ritual also bade, to each of the company, rheumatically; he had not yet seen Georges. The innkeeper moved to greet the newcomer. Georges Boutroux rose stealthily in his corner, and muttering to himself, "It never rains but it pours!" he began to creep by inches towards the neighbouring door.

The young workman was looking down at the floor, swinging his hands between his knees; the two grooms were gazing at the small cooking fire in the great open chimney—small as it was, it was oppressive in that weather; the lawyer-looking man was untying the napkin from his neck, having finished his meal: for the moment no one was looking at Georges.

He was up; he was out of the door quite silently, like a ghost, slipping behind his host's back; he was out the room in the winking of an eye, and already he had formed his plan.

He had seen outside the inn a chaise with lamps lit and hood up, and an ostler hooking the two horses' traces to the car. He divined that the lonely lawyer-like gentleman who had just completed his meal and seemed in some terror of democracy was on his way north. Georges' plan matured as he crept into the passage. He marvelled to find his mind working so quickly. He thought to himself, " It is a pity my uncle did not make me a solicitor or a thief, or something of that kind ; but I myself did not know my own aptitudes."

He slipped up the shadow of the house towards the stables.

It was as he imagined ; in a little harness-room, under the light of a swinging lamp, a postilion in shirt and drawers was drawing on his riding-breeches ; his yellow jockey cap and smart blue coat lay ready by him, as did his whip and gloves and his two jack-boots.

Boutroux came into that little room displaying in his outstretched fist a bunch of notes, and as he did so, said to the astonished fellow who stood ready to curse or cry out,—

" One hundred livres ; do you see ? If you will listen to me you will in a few moments be worth one hundred livres. If you interrupt me you will not have one." He pulled the assignats forth in a wad, got the man right in the eye with a steady look, and continued, " You are rider to the chaise to-night, and your post is Mirambeau."

The postilion, full of mystery and tasting adventure, said yes. He was a blue-eyed, tow-headed boy of perhaps eighteen years.

"Would you put your foot out that I may measure it with mine?" said Georges rapidly. The postilion did so. Georges' foot was a little the smaller. "I will keep my own boots," he said.

"I will dress in your clothes," said Georges in a rapid measure, "and you will dress in mine. See, in this coat of mine, I put this hundred livres. I will put on your clothes and cap, and walk out to the chaise in your clothes and mount. You shall follow me to see fair play. You shall follow in your shirt sleeves. I shall be holding my own coat with the hundred livres in it. You will hold the two horses' heads. In your own interests, you will not let them go until I hand you that coat, and also in your interests, and as you desire to keep what is in it when you have it, you will let the horses go. Do you understand? It is a check on either of us cheating— my family are in commerce, and I have learned such ways."

The postilion nodded. He did not understand, and he did not care. A hundred livres was an overwhelming sum, and he saw it there with his own eyes, staring him in the face.

The machinery of the transfer was perfected.

CHAPTER VI.

In which a Postilion goes Mad.

AT the door of the stable where it gave upon
the street, Boutroux, dressed in the postilion's clothes, with the postilion's large, peaked
hunter's cap drawn low over his eyes, and affect-
ing the postilion's swagger, advanced towards his
mount. The nervous professional man who had
been so silent during the altercation at the inn
was already hidden in the depths of the chaise,
for the showery thundery weather which still
threatened had caused his host to put up the
hood of it.

Boutroux mounted, with his discarded coat in
his hand. The fellow he had looted was standing
in his shirt sleeves holding the horses. He took
the coat, and let the horses go.

Boutroux caught the reins of the led horse
in his right hand, holding that hand gingerly
against his side, and wondering how the wound

would fare if the led horse pulled. But these old hack horses were like circus horses for training, he reflected, and like feather beds for slackness; and as soon as he was out in the darkness he would take the reins of both in his left hand.

He was supposed to know the road; at least, no instructions were given him. Georges had come from the north some half-dozen times in his young life, and he knew that his next stage would not be further than Mirambeau, and that there his fare would sleep. But he also knew that at Mirambeau there would be lights, and men acquainted with the work, and a dozen stable-fellows, perhaps, too much inclined to question a postilion. He had no intention of reaching Mirambeau.

It was perhaps half-past nine when he heard the order to start. Hardly was it given when the master of the house shouted after him an order to stop for some further directions or other which he had forgotten. Boutroux suddenly spurred the horse he was riding, the old thing bolted forward, and the light and rather rickety chaise was off at top speed, rolling dangerously upon the paved highroad.

To play the postilion is not an easy thing.

It is a trade by itself—half a gunner's and half a groom's. It has to do with horses—that is bad enough ; but also it involves some knowledge of the road. To play it as Boutroux desired to play it needed much more ; it needed a knowledge of things off the road as well, for on that main road he was determined he would not remain. He knew too well what might soon be behind him ! Once or twice as he sped on he thought that he heard some cry from his fare. He still spurred steadily forward, not sparing his cattle at the hills ; and he thought to himself, " What fare ever yet complained of a round speed ? " So he pressed forward.

The deluge of rain which had been threatening as they started broke upon them before Etaudiers. They clattered through the village —every light of the place out, and no witnesses to the drive—under a pouring and deafening shower ; and at Etaudiers it was—or, rather, just outside the village—that Boutroux's determination was taken.

Cross-roads may lead anywhere : they may end in ploughed fields, in dead walls, or in quarries ; and cross-roads at night may lead one straight to the devil. But Boutroux was going to risk it.

The barest glimmer of a road in the darkness leading to the right just outside Etaudiers determined him.

He spurred again, suddenly, so that with a heavy jolt the chaise lurched forward, and he found himself and it off the highway on a drenched earthen road, heavy going and almost impassable. He could feel the strain on the traces against his calves, but he urged the animals on, and somehow they stumbled through.

He had turned so sharp a corner that the rain beat now from the right side of the carriage and on the right flanks of the beasts, upon the right cheek of his face. The sudden passage from the paved highroad into the muddy land made a curious silence, in which one could hear the sough of the tired hoofs in the mud, even the very pattering of the rain. Boutroux was so intent upon his escape that he had almost forgotten the existence of the chaise behind him. He had quite forgotten the existence of his passenger, when he felt a very violent dig in the small of his back, and loud but inchoate sounds about "the wrong road" reached him through the roaring of the storm.

He set his teeth, shouted to his horses, and, as the going got a little drier at the top of a rise, compelled them to one further effort. The rain was gradually ceasing, the wind falling with it, and save the continual beat of his mounts' feet there was nothing to interrupt the protests now rising in violence from the unhappy man between the wheels, and he heard first a series of oaths, then two or three reasoned protests, then after a short silence a really frenzied appeal. But Etaudiers was not yet far enough away, and Boutroux still pressed on.

He had covered all but another league, in which he must have received some hundreds of heavy thrusts in the back unheeded, before the condition of his horses upon such a road gave him some reason to pause. He had gone from his starting-place at full speed for at least twelve miles. Hills which by the strict regulation of the law he was bound to walk he had taken at a canter on the highroad; for now some miles he had left that highroad for a country track on which no post-horse was warranted; and there were very evident signs in his own mount, and even in the led horse, that they had come to the end of their tether. He let them fall to a walk, and then at last the words of the gentleman who had commanded his services could be consecutively made out. Boutroux turned round with a pleasant smile, his young, handsome face lit strongly by the carriage lamps, pulled his beasts to a halt, and asked what might be the matter.

"The matter!" said the unfortunate lawyer. "The matter is, you dirty fool, that you will find yourself in jail with the break of day!"

Boutroux shook his head gently, and his smile was really beautiful in the lamp-light, had the exasperated traveller's mood only permitted him to appreciate its beauty. "Oh no," he said in a gentle manner, but (as he hoped) a little oddly. "Oh no; I shall not be in jail—I shall be in the Kingdom of my Father. It lies," he added ecstatically, "a little beyond the Hills of Gold."

"Good God!" cried the lawyer loudly. Then he muttered to himself, "I have to deal with a madman."

"Very far away," continued Boutroux, fixing him with large eyes in the lamplight as he turned half round, continuing his harangue and touching his horses to an easy walk—"very far beyond the Hills of Gold is the Kingdom of my Father —and it is there we ride, dear friend!"

His fare made but a dark mass against the hood of the carriage, and Boutroux, reflecting how pale and conspicuous his own face must be in the lamplight seen from the darkness, deliberately affected a most ecstatic air: his eyes turned upward under the heavy peak of his cap and sought his native skies as the tired horses plodded forward.

"Beyond the Hills of Gold," he said, "you will see these mortal beasts transformed, for my Father when He gave them to me gave them also wings, which they spread with the first rays of the morning; then shall your chariot also be turned into pure fire, and we will mount the skies."

The lawyer prided himself upon his knowledge of men and his rapidity of decision. He had seen things like this in the courts. It was really most unfortunate in the middle of the night . . . but there were ways of dealing with it.

"Monsieur the Prince-Postilion," he said, with profound deference in his tone, "I knew very well when I watched you mounting that you were not of earthly kind. I might have guessed that such as you would take me to the Blessed Realms. But since you did not tell me so in plain terms, why, I have come quite ill-accoutred and unprovided for that signal honour and for the Palace of the Skies. My clothes are drenched; I am fatigued; I have no change to speak of. I would not dare to enter the glories you propose to me until I am a little better groomed. Will you not, therefore, of your courtesy reach me the highroad again by the next turning? When we make Mirambeau, I have friends there who will put me into a proper suit of clothes, that I may continue my journey with you on to glory. There is a road," he added tentatively, "whereby we can reach the Land of the Blessed through Mirambeau; it is a shorter road."

"The Mirambeau to which we go," said Boutroux very gravely, " is another and a better Mirambeau, where the Bright Ones walk in peace that serve my Father." The horses went dumbly forward.

" I have always heard," answered the lawyer patiently, and with a mild, intelligent look, very sympathetic, and as though he quite understood the business—"I have always heard that the road to the Celestial City branches off about half a league from Mirambeau, beyond the square at the sign of The Pig That Spins."

Boutroux shook his head decisively. " You are quite wrong," he said with quiet firmness. "That *is* one road, but it is a long way round. I have promised," said he, "this very night to carry you into the Kingdom." Then changing his tone suddenly to one of the utmost ferocity, he added in a scream : "Bound and delivered ! Do you understand ? Fast bound !" He muttered fiercely, "And delivered—gagged."

He glared at his wretched fare as he said this, dropped his eyes again, and changing as suddenly back again to an extreme gentleness, he almost whispered, "Are you a lawyer, sir ?"

The passenger bethought him of a method which he had found very useful in a past crisis with a client whom he tamed.

"Yes, I am," he answered loudly and firmly, "and I can make you answer for your foolery ! "

"A lawyer ! " crooned the young man in a happy and inspired voice — "a lawyer ! The Man of Sin ! " Then he looked up and nodded affirmatively and gaily : "It's what I wanted ! You're the one "—his voice rose—"and you must get there bound and delivered : sealed, bound, and delivered ! "

For a quarter of an hour nothing further was said upon either side. Boutroux from time to time roared, laughed, and cursed to himself. The horses, too fatigued to canter or even to trot, wearily pulled the chaise along the now sandy road of the upland ; there was nothing but black and wholly silent night all round. Then the lawyer tried another ruse.

"Monsieur the Postilion," he said severely, " I am not worthy to enter that Kingdom. There is in Mirambeau a priest who will absolve me, and when I am shrived I will continue the journey with you."

Boutroux shouted to him without turning round,—

"Do not talk to me of Priests ; we will not hear of them in my Kingdom. A great fate is offered you, and you must take it whether or no. Besides which "—and here his voice suddenly rose again—"you are to be bound and delivered : I promised that ! Oh ! " he ended, smacking his lips, "you will be all the choicer served up in the midst of your sins."

"Monsieur the Postilion," said the lawyer, saying this time what was undoubtedly true, " I am in your hands."

He rapidly began to cast about for safety. There was no escape by wheedling or coaxing : he must get help from outside. He held his tongue, therefore, and as the chaise slowly rolled forward he waited for the dawn.

From early youth Boutroux had known how great an aid it was to the fatigue of travel to indulge in song ; during the next league and more of that slow progress, therefore, he sang.

Into snatches of tavern songs which were familiar to him, and some of which his unhappy fare recognised, he interpolated glorious gusts of prophecy—fierce, chaunted denunciations of the rich, little dancing refrains and visions of a world to come. From these in turn he would relieve himself by a loud whistling and occasionally by a well-chosen burst of maniacal laughter. After each of these he did not neglect to turn his face fiercely over his right shoulder, unlip a row of white teeth, and mutter at the man of law, " Bound and delivered ; mind that ! Trussed like a fowl,—and the choicer for your sins ! "

So he continued, working his instrument of fear, until at last far off upon the plain a very distant twinkling light threatened human habitation and danger. He drew rein and halted.

The wretched beasts shook and shivered though the damp night was warm ; a low and eerie wind blew in the scant trees which were here planted in a group by the roadside. Boutroux stiffly and deliberately dismounted.

" It is here," he said simply, " that I am to wait until the Messengers of the Kingdom meet us with the dawn." He lowered his head as he spoke thus, but kept his eyes lifted, fixed with a dreadful glare upon his victim, and made with his hands the firm gesture of a man who ties knots in cords and binds a prisoner.

"You are right," said the lawyer patiently; "I see the lights of their advance. I believe they are coming towards us. It might be wiser to go forward perhaps; it would be more courteous to greet them so."

"You are wrong!" said Boutroux decidedly, standing at his horses' heads, stiffly and in an expectant attitude. "It is against the rules. We have no rule or custom more observed in our society," he added in a louder voice, "than to wait at this sacred spot for orders; it is the gate of the Kingdom."

"I see," said the lawyer; "I understand."

For a good half-hour the pair remained there facing each other, the lawyer seated in his chaise with folded arms, flattering himself that with the day he would know how to deal even with such a case as this, Boutroux humming occasionally little snatches of songs, and then falling into silence or crooning happy prophecies of a delightful land, or describing in awful phrases the tortures that await wicked men.

In the east, to which the horses' bowed and

weary heads were turned, a faint glimmer of day began to be apparent. At first you could not tell whether it were not a mere paling of the stars or a glimmer of mist that was drifting before them ; but the light rose and grew, it smelt of morning, and very soon they were both of them aware of the dawn. They lapsed into a complete silence and watched it, each in his different mood.

When it was light enough for Boutroux to see the face of his companion he watched it narrowly, and perceived him to be exceedingly afraid.

The lawyer had got down from the chaise and was pacing backwards and forwards, slapping his hands upon his shoulders to keep warm in the chill of the dawning, and waiting until a somewhat broader day should enable him to take his measures. Had he been but a trifle more courageous, he would have closed with the lunatic ; but he was just not courageous enough, and that madman kept him steadily fixed with his eyes.

Under the growing light the landscape was now clear. Hedgeless fields, of stubble and crop alternately, stretched out infinitely upon every side. The lawyer stood apart with folded arms and glanced anxiously over those fields. The distant single light still glowed, a yellow patch, in the window of a farmhouse a mile away, and sure enough, two men and a woman, with the implements of labour carried over their shoulders, were proceeding from it towards the harvest land.

"I think," said the lawyer tentatively, watching the effect of his words—"I think these are the messengers of your Father?"

"I have no doubt," answered Boutroux in a low, grave, and reverent voice; "I know them, and they will soon be here."

"It is only reasonable," said the lawyer, "that I should meet them." He began the first few steps towards the fields, tremulously, not knowing how the move might strike the cunning of his ravisher. He was overjoyed to find that his escape was approved. And just as he got out of earshot he heard Boutroux's loud tone telling him with decision to announce the advent of the young Heir with his Winged Horses, his Man of Sin, and his Chariot of Fire.

The lawyer was not accustomed to damp fields even upon a light soul; he was not in a mood to negotiate them easily. He pressed forward feverishly over the six or seven hundred yards that separated him from succour: he did not dare cry out until many minutes had passed, and until he was not only within hail of the peasants, but nearer to them than to his very formidable postilion. When he judged that such action was safe, he cried out at the top of his voice for help.

The group of peasants stopped; they saw the post-chaise, the official uniform of the postilion's distant figure; they remembered that the law compelled them to lend re-mounts for a breakdown, and without a moment's hesitation they turned and ran in an opposite direction, lest such a sacrifice should be required of them. After them ran the lawyer, and as a stern chase is a long one, it was perhaps another quarter of an hour before his frenzied appeals reached them in any understandable shape. When they saw that something more than an ordinary breakdown was toward, they turned and awaited him. He came up with them. He was haggard with the experience of that dreadful night, drenched, most unhappy, and almost breaking down with physical fatigue; the clods were heavy on his thin, buckled shoes, and in general he presented that lamentable spectacle of a well-to-do man in distress — a spectacle always intensely agreeable to the poorer classes, but more especially delightful when they see a chance to profit by it. As he came up to them, he panted out,—

"Gentlemen, I implore you! Madame, I implore you! A dreadful thing has happened: a man has gone mad!"

They looked at him stolidly, and did not answer.

"Gentlemen," he said again, "I implore you in Christian charity! Madame, a man has gone mad! It is but your duty to help me bind him and to restore him to his people!"

"What man?" said the leading peasant suspiciously. The lawyer had now come up with them, and was standing face to face.

"My driver!" he continued, gasping. "He has gone mad, and calls himself a son of heaven; and he has landed me in this dreadful place! I must require your help. I must require it in the name of the law. People of importance await me to-day in Niort."

"Oh, there's nothing dreadful about our place," said the woman shrewishly; "you must be a little more civil in your speech. We are not in the time of the lords, remember." She looked at him suspiciously. "What brought you here?"

"That chaise," the lawyer answered foolishly

enough, "that accursed chaise, and its devil of
a driver."

The peasant whom he had first addressed watched
him for a moment in silence. "I see nothing in
your story," he said brusquely, and noting with
suspicion the crumpled broadcloth of the wealthier
man. "It's you that seems a little unsettled. If
there has been a breakdown your postilion will
know how to find help : it is his business."

"You do not understand," said the lawyer;
"he is mad ! he is unfortunately run *mad !*
He called me the Man of Sin."

"Well, there is a method in his madness,"
said the peasant with a grin, "and he seems to
be taking a better course than you for finding
proper succour." He pointed with his finger
over his interlocutor's shoulder. The lawyer
turned round, and at once began waving his
arms in frenzy and shouting, for what he saw
was this : the chaise standing, horseless and
alone upon the way, and very far off upon
the edge of the countryside, just turning into
a wood that fringed the horizon, the postilion
upon his mount, with the led horse following.
Even at that distance he could see that the led
horse went reluctantly, wearied beyond measure
with such a series of madcap adventures.

A moment later, the unhappy lawyer had no occasion now to continue his shouting and his gestures. The insane postilion had disappeared into the woods, and he was there with the peasants in the bare plain alone.

How he bargained with them for a mount to take him to the nearest post upon the high-road, how they fleeced him, how he threatened vengeance, how upon that account other men, labouring in the fields, surrounded him and showed the new temper of democracy, how he was compelled to swear that he had no title, but was an honest patriot, and how at last—at the cost of all the ready money upon him—he obtained a very stubborn old she-donkey and a cow to pull his vehicle back to Etaudiers, would be of entertainment to any history concerning his adventures, but they have nothing to do with Boutroux, who was by this time in the depths of the high wood, and for the moment saved.

CHAPTER VII.

In which a Sack of Charcoal is taken and a Girl is left.

BOUTROUX'S vague knowledge of the country told him that he might not be far from Chiersac. Once well into the high wood (for the earthen country road soon became a wandering track therein) he dismounted and patted his poor mount upon the neck.

"It is a thousand pities," he said, fondling him, "that you should have to suffer so much for me! But what would you? Men in necessity ill-use their own kind, let alone dumb brutes. I have no oats for you," he added sadly, as the two patient beasts stretched out their heads towards him, and one of them took a gentle bite at his sleeve, "but there's plenty of grass."

He mercifully took the bits from their mouths and strapped them by the buckle to the rings of the harness. He saw that the loops of the traces were tied up high, so that the leather should not drag and hamper the animals in their going ; he loosened the girth of the saddle on the near horse to give him ease ; he slipped the irons up, so that if he felt inclined to roll he should do himself no harm. And having done these things he made his horses a little speech, saying,—

"Good horses, I am an exile ; and I must confess it to you who have never told lies in your life, that within the last twenty-four hours I have told some hundreds of lies : but," he added, sighing, "it was fate!" And as he said it one of the horses neighed.

"Precisely," continued Boutroux; "that is the way I feel about it too. There are times when a man must lie. And now, horses, I must dismiss you. Do not follow me. You may have observed from my actions perhaps (though you horses are stupid beasts) that I was not keen on being followed during these last few hours of my life. Go," he concluded gently, "find your way home. Even if you cannot do it you will be stolen by some other of my human sort ; and since horses are always serviceable, you will be more sure of food than I."

He strode into the underwood. For a yard or two the poor brutes made as though to follow him.

"I hate to do it, but with sheer stupidity genius itself cannot argue!" he thought, and lifting a piece of dead wood that lay there he threw it at his former friends. Both looked astonished, one a little hurt. They turned from him, and browsing the coarser grass beneath the trees, made vaguely for home.

The sun had risen, the heat was increasing. The insects of August buzzed drowsily in the wood, and content came upon the young man again as it had come upon him when he had landed from the boat upon the northern shore of the Gironde twenty-four hours before. His fatigue also came upon him so strongly that he fell, stupidly happy, under the low branch of a short oak, and dropped at once into a profound and satisfying sleep.

As Boutroux slept he dreamed. He dreamed a curious dream—vivid and yet mixed with memory.

It seemed to him in his dream that he was still in that wood, but that the wood was home; and that in some way it was upon the fringe of a kingdom, and that the kingdom belonged to his people and his line. He thought he saw himself going through the wood for hours and hours, and as he went he spoke to beasts that passed him—

wild deer and the birds of the greenwood, and
little rabbits that were not afraid, and squirrels in
the branches, and now and then a horse grazing
at random. And it seemed to him that these
answered him in various manners—pleased or
unpleased, shy, pert, grave, humorous, angered,
or loving—as might men. It seemed to him that
he was conscious as he walked—that he divined
very well—how every step he took he was taking
deeper and deeper into some kingdom of his own,
and yet farther and farther away from a dear home
and things he knew. He felt like an exile who
happened also to be upon a pilgrimage.

Just as he was coming out of that wood of his
dream and half saw, or thought he saw, a very
glorious landscape beyond, in which, in some odd
way, was resumed all that he had lost and all that
he should find, he stirred, his mind lost ease; that
landscape resolved itself into a mist and confusion
of sunlight shining through green boughs. The
outlines of those boughs grew precise, and he
woke suddenly to this world. He sat bolt upright
and stared with seeing eyes, first at the real things
about him, then inwards at his fate. He began to
revolve the same.

"Boutroux," said he gravely, "in the next lie
you tell you must either lie freely as should a

citizen in the third year of Liberty, or constrainedly : for if you are dressed anyhow—even as a pauper—you will be free to lie freely ; but if you are dressed as a postilion you will be constrained to lie constrainedly, having to lie up to your clothes as it were, as do dukes and politicians and patriots, and scum of that kind. Boutroux, since lie you must, I prefer you should lie as a free man ; therefore you must get rid of this postilion's garb. Boutroux," he added, "there are some who would be puzzled what to do, well knowing that men naked are fallen upon by the guard and thrust into prison, knowing also that men must see their fellow men in villages or towns if they are to live, and knowing that in such places are guards especially to be found— game-keepers and police, and chance patrols and authorities. A foolish man, Boutroux, might think it impossible to get out of such a dilemma, either to go as a postilion or to go naked—and either is fatal. But you, Boutroux, have more mastery, I hope, over your fate ! "

He first took off his coat and carefully turned it inside out. He was delighted to note that the lining was black. He next pulled off his postilion's knee-breeches, turned them inside out, and found the lining of those to be black also. "That," he said gravely, "is as it should be." The black coat and the black knee-breeches (as they now were) he carefully donned again, and began to consider his next act. He bethought him of his cap.

"To wear no headgear is eccentric, but no man is imprisoned for it," he said, "while to wear a postilion's cap is to be a postilion."

From the pocket of his coat, now turned inside out against his shirt, he drew a matchbox and tinder. With these he lit a little fire of dry twigs, whereon most thoughtfully he burned his cap ; and as it burned he said to it,—

"Not because you are a heretic, my cap, do I burn you—for the Rights of Man have done away with all that—but because you will not conform with the rest of your society. Who can wear a yellow postilion's cap with black clothes ? Burn, and may God have mercy on your soul !"

His spurs he unbuckled, and put them into that inner pocket. Then taking the ash of the little fire whereon he had immolated his head-gear, he deliberately smeared it upon his face and hands, and quenching a coal of it in a puddle of dirty water hard by, he rubbed the black streaks of the char upon his forehead and round his mouth. "If I had a mirror," he murmured, "I would make it as it should be, and every stroke would tell. But as it is I must do what bad artists do, and must trust to blur." With these words he rubbed hard at the streaks he had drawn, so as to mix them with the remaining ashes on his face; he was careful to blacken round the eyes especially, that the whites might show clear, and round the lips that the teeth might be equally apparent.

"In this way," he said, "men know a charcoal burner." And where a speck of white thread appeared upon the seams of the black lining which he now wore inside out, he rubbed it with the same charred stick to darken it.

Having done all these things it occurred to him that the old proverb "Who sleeps dines" was especially true in this, that he who wakes is hungry. He had not eaten since his snack of the evening before, and he was a little puzzled to know how a charcoal-burner could earn a living where, for all he could see, no charcoal had ever been made since the beginning of the world; but he noted that the wood about him had beech trees in it, and as he sniffed the air he thought he caught a smell of smouldering. So he went forward in hope and faith for charcoal-burners' heaps.

"It is one thing," thought Boutroux, "to cover

one's tracks, and it is another thing to earn one's living ; but to do the two together is well-nigh impossible."

So musing he pushed through the undergrowth, following the ancient rule that one should on a high land always go down-hill if one would seek man, till in half an hour or so he came suddenly out of that dense growth on to a sunlit meadow where a stream trickled from the dampness of the wood which he had just left.

Hardly was he twenty yards on, over the pleasant grass, when a young girl, fresh, beautiful, and strong, with her pail balanced in her right hand and her left arm akimbo, called to him from a gate far off,—

"Charcoal-burner, we shall need a sack ! "

"God is in it," said Boutroux piously. "I thought as much : they do make charcoal in this wood. It will go hard if I make none with them." He shouted roughly back, "When, Beauty ? "

"Never if you talk like that," she said ; "but before night if you would wish to see my father's money, you may tell your dirty gang."

He smiled at her with the whiteness of his teeth upon his blackened face ; she smiled at him, and he went back into the forest.

5

"Heaven," said he as he got into the high wood again, "who has provided charcoal-burners unexpectedly, and a wench and her father for customers, will not allow this sparrow to fall unnoticed to the ground. But from what I know of Heaven it will not teach me how to burn charcoal; and even if it did, for all I know the process may be one of weeks—and though I am willing to steal, yet, God help me! I have no sack."

It is related of Ulysses that the extremity of evil was but a spur to him, and opportunity a gate of delivery. It shall be related of Boutroux that whether it was his youth or his good fortune or the gods that smile on exiles, something would always suggest to him what a man should do; and so it was upon that day and in that hour, for he said to himself, "Since there are charcoal-burners, how should they be found? By their folly and the folly of other men, as human things are always found!" And having come to that conclusion, and seeing that the girl had gone indoors again, he crept carefully under the cover of the wood towards a more distant farm which lay upon the edge of the greenery, and when he got there he saw a young man digging with a spade in the garden-patch, and he said to him,—

"I've come for the money for that sack of charcoal."

"We've had no sack of charcoal," said the lad roughly. "Who sent you?"

"My mates," said Boutroux as roughly.

"You can go back and tell your fools of mates that they have mistaken the house, or that you have." And the boy went on digging. But as he plunged his spade vigorously into the earth he was inspired to add, "Besides which, they have no right to be burning at the White Cross, for that is village land."

"It is not," said Boutroux in the challenging tone of one who had studied the ground and known the spot for years.

"It is," said the young man, looking up and sweating in that heat, his eyes angry under his wet brows. "It's village land two hundred toises from the edge of the wood all round. The White Cross marks it, and they're on this side of it!"

"In a manner of speaking," said Boutroux cautiously, "they are."

"Well," said the other triumphantly, "there you are! Pace the path and see if it's not within the two hundred toises! I'll come with you." And as he said it he came through the wicket of the hedge across which they had been talking and began measuring strides along a widening path through the underwood.

"I was only joking," said Boutroux hurriedly. "I know it's village land. I didn't mean to rile you," he added good-humouredly, "but I did think it was here I was to come for the money."

"Well, it isn't," said the young man a little mollified and turning back to his digging. "It's in hell for all I know, but it isn't here."

"It must be somewhere about," muttered Boutroux, and he disappeared down the path.

It led him, as he had expected, to an open clearing, and in that clearing he saw the stack of faggots, the little hut of turf, the cut stumps, and the signs of past dead fires which mark the burning of charcoal in a wood.

How often in another day, as a child walking with his nurse in the woods of home near the city, he had seen such camps, but never had he wondered till now exactly how the trade was run. Nor did he continue to wonder about that or to care about it when once his eyes had fallen upon a large sack full of that which was to him at the moment more precious than gold, but unfortunately it served as a pillow for a huge and sleeping man.

This giant was snoring in the noonday rest: one arm was under his head to shield his face from the rough edges of the charcoal in the sack, the other lay listless along his side. Beside him a leathern bottle of wine half emptied, and a loaf which had formed his meal, lay at random.

"My dear grandmother," said Boutroux in his heart, "who died three years ago, used always to tell me that I should choose business before pleasure, and she would add, 'where you think you have an equal choice so far as duty is concerned, take the more difficult course and you will be right.' It is therefore," he sighed, "my business first to shift that sack, and only if I accomplish that successfully shall I have any right to steal this wine and bread. It is by attention to things in their right order that men prosper."

There is a game called spillikins, in which a man wins by moving a number of delicate ivory spills intertwined one with another, and by moving them in such a manner that he separates them without shaking any one by the movement of its neighbour. This, on a larger scale, was Boutroux's task.

He began wisely enough by giving the charcoal sack a vigorous kick so that the sleeper's head bumped heavily against the ground. His snore was suddenly interrupted and caught in a violent spasm within the convolutions of his head; he gasped, squirmed as though he would wrestle with the ground, then oddly sighed again, rolled on his back, and let his great arms spread out in the shape of a cross; his head fell back stark against the earth, and in a moment was snoring again.

Boutroux looked at him with wonderment. "If you had woken," he said, "you would have compelled me to yet another lie. . . . I have carried nothing heavy, though I have often boasted of it and lied in clubs. But you, my charcoal sack, be light to me. I should imagine from what I know of the stuff that it wasn't a patch upon wheat for weight."

Saying this he very silently and gingerly crouched down, slung the burden upon his shoulder, and finding it bearable began to stagger off, when suddenly he remembered something.

"A man does not live by charcoal alone," he muttered.

He crept back in that noontide heat and over the coarse grass without a sound, avoiding every twig, and holding his very breath for silence: he lifted the huge round loaf and the gourd of wine most tenderly as though they were young children whom he loved, got his sack upon his back again, with his free left hand, and made down the path towards the hamlet and the two farms. He had heard that labouring men slept at noon for but a short while: nevertheless he halted upon the edge of the wood, hastily ate a slice of the bread and drank a gulp of the wine, recognised when he had satisfied himself that it was wiser to restore them, went back and laid them where he had found them; returned, took up his charcoal sack again, and bore it across the meadow towards the gate where he had seen the young girl in her beauty and her strength, holding the pail balanced with her arm akimbo.

"Now I could have drawn that," said Boutroux, looking at the now empty landscape, the gate, the wall, the small white farmhouse, and the falling open valley below. "I could have drawn it, but if I had, what good would that have been to me? It is my business to deliver this sack of charcoal to the farmer. He needs the sack and I the money. Nay, he has positively ordered the sack, and I have been at very great pains to obtain it. This is commerce: this is as it should be: this is exchange. Here are two citizens satisfied."

With this he had come up to the house, and he knocked at the door of it, slipped down his sack upon the big threshold stone, leant negligently against the door-post and waited until they should open from within. While he so waited he considered to himself how excellent had been his meal; and he made a rule which he then determined firmly to keep the whole of his life, which was this: never to take wine if he could help it without bread, and still more surely never to take bread if he could possibly help it without wine.

He heard steps within: the door opened, and in the cool dark room which it disclosed he saw the girl who had been the cause of all this labour, and from whom he hoped to receive its corresponding reward.

CHAPTER VIII.

*In which a Sack of Charcoal is left
and a Girl is taken.*

THE girl came forward from within the house
to the door ; her beauty was veiled by the
darkness of the room, her upstanding figure was
free, and Boutroux said within his heart that
the circumstance of man was unworthy to the
dignity of love. He regretted for a moment
the charcoal with which he had rubbed his face,
and the work upon which he chanced by fate
to be engaged. He stood looking at her with a
smile which under other circumstances would have
been half ironical and half adventurous, but which
appearing as a white row of teeth framed in that
new black face of his was startling rather than subtle.

"Why the devil can't you carry the sack on
your shoulders ? " she said by way of greeting.
"Have I cleaned that threshold stone for nothing ? Great brute ! "

Boutroux did not understand, but he understood when she put into his hand a silver piece in earnest of payment.

"Pick it up!" she shouted like a young commander; "pick it up, and go round to the back."

He hoisted the sack upon his shoulder again, making as though it were a great burden, and awaited her orders, bent beneath his burden. But he affected strength by looking up brightly as he did so, his white teeth gleaming again against the darkness of his dirty skin, and his eyes the brighter for such a background.

"You're not one of those who brought it before," she said.

"Not I," he answered richly. "I am plying three trades just now: to the one I am fast becoming used, which is wandering; to the second, which is charcoal-burning, I am but a very new hand; the third I have known and practised most thoroughly for now three years, and I thought myself a master at it," he continued, swinging the bag over his other shoulder by way of a rest, and drawing himself up so that she marvelled how he could bear the weight of it in such an attitude. "I thought myself a master at it; but as one lives one learns. . . ."

"What is that third trade of yours?" she said.

"It is a form of hunting," he answered; "it is a kind of hunting in which the hunter himself is always wounded, and even the hare does not usually escape a wound."

"That," said the girl as she strode by his side, short-kilted, and already amused, "is a proverb of your village. We do not know it here."

"I shall be happy to expound its full meaning in good time," said Boutroux from beneath his sack.

The girl said nothing in reply, but abruptly: "My father keeps his charcoal in a barn he has. I will take you to that barn." And she did so, but not by the shortest road.

"It is a proverb of my village," he answered, after thinking a little while, "and I myself have never quite understood it; we have it in another form. We say that in that hunting the joy is all at the beginning, before the chase is up, and the sadness all at the end, and the worse for successful ending. But we say that either way there is no weariness in that hunting."

"You learnt that proverb also, I think," she said with a good laugh, "in your own country. We have no such proverb here."

"Well then," said he, forgetting the path and

everything but her, "have you this proverb, 'In that hunting the quarry knows the hunter better than the hunter knows the quarry'?"

"No," said she.

"Or have you this: 'The quarry fears the huntsman, but the huntsman fears the quarry more'?"

"No," said she again stubbornly, "this would seem to be spoken of the hunting of wolves and of wild boars, which doubtless swarm in that wild bad land of yours. For no other beast turns upon him that hunts or tries to rend him."

"Young lady," said Boutroux with great courtesy, as he shifted his sack again to the other shoulder a little more wearily, "first let me tell you that the path is getting long ; and secondly, let me tell you that the quarry of which I speak *does* turn and rend the hunter. It is its nature so to do."

"But is the chase not wounded too?" she said.

"Oh, child," he answered, sighing, "have I not told you that both are wounded? Hunter and hunted too!"

"Never yet," she said in a lower tone, "has any charcoal-burner called me a child."

"And never yet," he answered in a tone yet

lower than hers, "has any child, however beautiful, called me a charcoal-burner."

They had come to the end of a field, where a slovenly gate led the path round and through to other paddocks of the croft. The moment was propitious for a halt in their little journey. The sun in its early afternoon decline was at once hot and beneficent. She looked at him under the shade of her great hair, and asked him whether the burden were not heavy, and whether he would not rest a moment.

"It is very heavy!" he said, and slipped it to the ground as if it were indeed of a great weight; and then he sat down beside it, his legs stretched out, his back resting upon the burden, and his eyes looking up at hers as she stood above him.

"Charcoal-burner," she said, "I have known no charcoal-burners come to my father's house, though they come so often during the charcoal-burning days, who seemed so little fitted to their trade as you. Now, if you have something that you are not saying and that you would wish to say, say it, and I will keep faith; for I know very well that this forest is sometimes a refuge in days like ours."

When she had said this she watched him

with a little smile, looking for a new look in his eyes ; and he, putting on an appearance of due sadness, said,—

"Young lady, it is not one hour since I met you, and yet the thing I have to say is very near my heart."

She went a little further off, and leaned against the gatepost, still looking down at him.

"Charcoal-burner," she said, "you are not a charcoal-burner at all, for you speak like the men in the cities."

"Will you hear what I have to say ?"

"Certainly," said she, half humbly.

"It is this," he answered. "I have now been loose and flying, not without fear, for a day and for half a day, and in all that time and in all this heat I have had but three hours of sleep, and one bottle of good and two subsequent gulps of raw wine ; and I do most earnestly beseech you by my patron Saint, St. George as he once was — for God knows his status nowadays—that you will bring me that cool refreshment and drink which your kind face should promise me."

When she had gazed at him for a little while, smiling less strongly, but not wholly ceasing to smile, she said at last : "I will bring it you, though you have burned no charcoal—no, nor anything, I think, in all your life but things you had no right to burn."

She turned her back upon him and strode off resolutely across the meadows in a direction she knew, while Boutroux lay there, not unhappily, and considered the largeness of the world.

"It is evident," he murmured to himself, "that proper adventure and a change in things, large acquaintance and refreshment of every kind, lie open before the feet of any man whatsoever that chooses to travel. I could have wished," he added silently in his heart, "that my occasion for travel had been a little more genial, for every man has roots to him, and mine are all dragged out of the earth to-day, for ever. But Lord, the largeness of the world!"

As he so pondered in that happy and mellowing sunlight, he glanced drowsily here and there, through half-shut lids, at the meadows and the highland hedges and the more distant woods. It was very still, a crowd of midges was buzzing over the brookland below, and already the grasshoppers had begun their loud chirping in the roots of the aftermath. Nature was full and pleased; he was content to fix those drowsy, half-shut eyes of his upon an edge of the near woodland where a bird and its mate walked and hopped oddly together, picking for sustenance in the leaf mast, and helping one another. The one walked proudly, the other with seduction ; the one was brave, he thought, in the eyes of its mate, and its mate, he imagined, in the eyes of the brave one, beautiful. Nay, the beauty of the one and the courage of the other, in some way communicated themselves to his mind : he blessed the two birds and wished them happiness. But even as he did so, some movement of his, or some approach of another animal in the underwood, frightened them, and first the male, glancing round by way of guard, gave a little cry, then his mate rose, and both together took the broad heaven and flew.

"It was a pretty sight," thought Boutroux, "and now they are off to the sky." He would have carried his thought further had not that girl with whose conversation he had so lately been filled, appeared near by with a flagon in either hand. She had come through some opening in the hedge and he had not noticed her.

He rose to his feet with some gallantry, though a little stiffly after such adventures, and tried to take her burden from her. She put both flagons resolutely behind her back, and said : "How do you know that they are yours ?"

"I do not know," he said, "but I am very thirsty."

"Why, then," she answered pleasantly, "you shall be satisfied. Have you no mug or glass?"

"I have none," he replied with great courtesy of inclination and of gesture, "and if you will not drink first I will not drink at all."

"My mother told me once," said the girl, "that women must not drink wine."

"There is something in that," said Boutroux; "your mother was a wise woman. And what did she say of water?"

"Oh, one may drink water; but I am not thirsty. Nevertheless, since you need companionship, I will drink both wine and water with you."

When she had said this, she looked in his face, and in her soul she felt that the lines of it, and the strength of the eyes, and the laughter in the mouth were something that she would know and need. She drank from the one flagon and from the other in the Spanish fashion, and handed them to him.

"From which did you drink last?" he asked.

"From the water," said she.

"Then I will drink from that first," he answered, taking a long draught therefrom. "And now"— catching the wine from her before she was aware

—" I will drink the wine in order to remember your name by it."

" But I have not told you my name," she said.

" Nor need you," he answered, " for I know it already, and from now onwards I shall know it all my life."

When they had so drunk wine and water together in a sort of sacramental way, they said nothing more. He lifted his sack again, caring nothing whether it seemed light or heavy, nor willing to make believe before her or to deceive her any longer. But he went forward through the further small paddock along the path towards a rude strong hut of hewn logs that stood there, wherein was a store of charcoal, and in the dark recesses of it a sort of pen where a beast might stand, and in the pen dry fern litter that smelled well, and a little straw scattered over it, clean and good. He opened the sack and poured out its contents upon the charcoal heap.

" There," said he, " is the end of my tale."

" You shall be further paid for it," she said.

" You can pay me best," he answered, " with a little lodging, if it is safe that I should lodge here. The weather is warm, and, if you will believe me, I need concealment."

She asked him suddenly: "What is your name?"

"It is odd that you should ask me my name," he answered at once, and in quite another tone, "for your name I should never have asked. Have I not told you that I should never forget your name for all my life?"

"But you do not know it," she answered again in a low voice, and very troubled.

"Oh yes," said he, speaking in the manner of the river Garonne when it runs at night with so sincere and so profound a noise, a noise so slight and yet proclaiming so great a depth and volume; "I know your name. After a few moments I knew it for ever and ever."

This young woman, full of health and of the woods, in her eighteenth year as I have heard, a companion to the lads of the village, and an exchanger of taunts with the charcoal-burners of the forest, the stay of her father's house (for he was a widower), and the nurse and the upbringer of children younger than herself, had a face designed for some great moment.

She had never known how swiftly the gods may descend and strike, nor in what manner revelations come; nor could she tell how little these great things may have to do with a complexion or an accident of feature, or with vesture, or with anything at all but the body that men bear and the soul that makes it all. From that moment in her poverty she knew as much as ever has been known, and when she left him she said to him,—

" Whatever you may be, lie there close in concealment ; for I alone of all the household fetch and carry, and I will feed you, and I will preserve you. And God deal with me as I deal with you. You say that you know my name : I do not know your name, nor will I ask it, friend."

When she had said this she hurriedly left that hut and took the meadows back towards her home ; but though she had said that while he knew her name, she did not know his, yet in her eyes now was something sprung from him which no length of years would quite extinguish.

When she had gone, Georges Boutroux in the hut again considered, but in a very different mood, the vastness of this world. The place seemed a prison to him, and, as is the nature of prisons, he dared not break it. It called for companionship, as prisons will ; but again, as prisons do, it suggested only one companionship.

He was very greatly fatigued, he had done more than a man should do in every way ; he considered first what relief might be before him, and what opportunity for getting clean away. Next, and more drowsily as he fell back upon the fern litter and the straw, whether his trick with the charcoal had yet angered the charcoal-burners' camp, and whether they also were perhaps upon him. Lastly, as the good sleep came down upon him like a happy mist, he wandered confusedly among the inward parts of his soul, counting that last hour and dwelling in it, and forgetting all the wild dance of the two days. He knew that it was something newer than ever he had known before. Then he saw the face and heard the voice so that it was already the beginning of a dream : he heard the low voice and he saw the sunburned face that was the woods and the spirit of them, and he saw the small hands holding from such arms the promise of refreshment and of peace. But after this even the beginnings of his dream left him, and he fell contentedly into his sleep.

CHAPTER IX.

In which a Lover finds himself in the Dark.

THE summer night upon the uplands and on the borders of the woods is cold : there is dew upon the grass, and in the open sky a chilliness which even the cattle feel in their byres, so that they crouch down upon the litter, or, if they are folded in the open, gather together for warmth.

But Boutroux was not cold : in that long sleep of his he knew a great contentment with which warmth was mingled, and his sleeping and half-dreaming brain imagined permanent satisfaction. For many hours he lay thus upon the straw above the fern litter in the dark refuge of the hut : when he woke, he woke so refreshed that he seemed for a moment in a new life ; he remembered nothing—but bit by bit the rapid story of his quarrel, his exile, and his flight returned to him. He drew himself up upon his soft bed ; he found above him a rough and thick but good covering of wool which some one while he slept had gently laid there, and new straw heaped about his feet and knees. It was very early morning.

Everything smelt of morning, and the grey quiet light which came through the door of the shed and through the chinks of its woodwork proclaimed the hour before the sun. The little beasts of the woodland and the grass were already astir; save for their movement there was no noise. He raised himself yet further, he found his arm less stiff; he unfastened the bandage, it came off easily and the surface of the wound was healed.

"It is wonderful," said Boutroux to himself, "what contentment and good novelty will do to a man! They will close up his very flesh, and certainly they restore his soul."

Having so thought on the matter, he rose sharply from the fern litter and the straw, shaking them about him with a small noise. He coughed to clear his throat, and he had begun some sort of little song to cheer him, when he heard a low "Hush!" and peering into the darker corner of the shed before him, he saw there the figure of his sleeping and his dreams.

She was leaning blotted out in the shadow

against the wooden wall. Her arms were crossed upon her firm young breast. Her milking-pails and the yoke to which they were fastened stood upon the ground at her feet. The very faint light, reflected from the bright straw on to her visage, just barely showed its lineaments ; but he divined her eyes. She did not speak, but whispered,—

"Speak low. I have been here waiting for near an hour, lest you should be betrayed."

Boutroux approached her without any noise. She uncrossed her arms as he came and clasped her hands before her. He took her left hand and kissed it gently, and he thought, even in that half light, that her colour rose as he lifted his face to hers.

"There are several who would find you," she said again in a whisper, "but they cannot guess where you are, for they have been told nothing and they believe you to have fled. Only I warn you : and for that reason I rose while it was yet dark and came to watch until you were awake. But I would not waken you, for you suffered from a great fatigue ; and in your sleep, both in the night and now, you laughed and were taken with fever."

"It was you," he said, "who came in the night

and put this cloth over me against the dampness and the cold, and it was you who put the straw about my feet and knees."

"It was I," she answered. "Here we keep much of the husbandry, and often my pails are left here for the milking,—so none could wonder."

"Nor do I wonder," he answered, "and I have better reason than they to understand."

As he said this to her, she lifted one arm a moment as though to lay it on his shoulder, but she let it fall again and would not. "Very soon," she said, "they will be all astir."

A cock crowed somewhere in the hamlet below; he crowed a deep, gay note, full-hearted in his pride and challenging. In the high farm that was her father's he was answered shrilly by some young adventurous rival; a third in the neighbouring croft took up the call. As those two heard these sounds, they heard also the hoofs of horses moving over the pavement of a stable far off, and the chink of iron; and there came the whistling of a lad on his way to the fields and labour.

"You will stay here," she said. "You must not move, and you must trust me. I will bring you food."

"There will never be a time," he said, "that you may come, whether you bring me food or no, but I shall feed. And even when you are not here, I shall feed in a fashion upon a shade."

She would not answer him. She put the yoke upon her graceful shoulders so that they were bent to her labour, she straightened herself and swung the pails and went out to the field, short-kilted, walking strongly and with the morning upon her. He saw her for but a moment as she passed the door, but almost immediately, as she left him, there came palely through that same entry the first ray of the sun ; it bore with it a sort of miraculous enlivenment and a changing of all things as it came. And Boutroux thought to himself again :—

"Undoubtedly these are great days ! " Then he considered all that she had told him—how she had told him to lie close and to speak to none, and how she would visit him again.

An hour later she re-entered, calling carelessly over her shoulder to companions far off, and saying that when she had left her pails in the shed she would rejoin their company. She put down her burdens swiftly, and came to him where he in-habited his lonely place, and set before him in a hurried way a paper wherein there was cold meat and household bread, dark in colour, and a little salt.

"I have no wine," she said in a low voice.

"Be pleased to hear," he answered more deliberately, but in a voice as low, "that I cannot drink wine of a morning, having in my time drunk more than should be drunk at night ; but since it is you have brought this meat to me, there will be wine enough in it, I think, and in the bread as well."

She was gone immediately, so that none outside could have wondered at her delay ; and as she went out she called again to her companions, saying that the shed was too far a place to leave the pails in, and for the future she would borrow a neighbour's barn nearer to their own byres.

Meanwhile, Boutroux in his hiding all day long waited for the evening, and was as patient as his strength permitted him to be.

The sun had fallen to its afternoon : he was feeling drowsy with such enforced indolence and secrecy, when, before he was aware of it, she was at his side again, bringing this time wine with the bread and meat. She spoke with less content and more hurriedly than before ; she begged him not to move nor to make one sound until it should be dark, for he was in danger ; she promised him when it was dark to return and to tell him the story of his danger. And once more he obeyed her.

The evening of that day fell : the sounds of labour retired and were silenced, the grasshoppers after their loud evening chirping reposed, for the night chilled them. And Boutroux waited until it seemed to him that sleep had come down upon the hamlet and the charcoal-burners, and all the living things of the woodland and the clearing. As he so waited, he heard again the step which he now knew like his own name, and she was by him ; but she bore nothing save her message.

Her voice, which had been hurried and troubled when she had last brought him succour, was now more troubled and more hurried ; the tale she had to tell him was the tale he knew—for she, too, knew it now. And as she began to tell him his own story, coming slowly to it, and hesitating, she held him once involuntarily, and held him close, to complete her telling of it, and she spoke to him in a terror which was a great and a proud thing for him to hear ; for as he felt its source he himself could not be at all afraid—no, not even of those things that pursue a soul in darkness. And as for the pursuit of men—hearing her low voice and considering her care, he gloried in that peril.

Her speech was halting : she told him the

last things first, so that he must question her gently, almost as by caresses. He thought she trembled, though she was so strong and well-poised.

"They neither know me nor where I am," he said.

"Friend," she whispered to him, "you said in that first speech of ours—which, oh my God, is surely all my life ago!—that you were a hunter at times."

"All men are hunters at times," he said.

"Friend," she said, "when some brave thing is hunted and the hounds come upon it, not only in chase but on flank and flank, it goes hard with that quarry."

"It is the end of it," he answered tenderly, "or, at any rate, it is the end of that hunting."

"But," she said, with a little sob and laugh at his perpetually turning her phrase, "this hunting is no hunting of lovers, and they have you in chase and on either flank as well, for I will tell you :—This morning as I left you with the pails to go milking, I met no one, for the hour was early, only Peter in the hollow, the son of the man they call Rich Hamard, who has the main croft and farms the taxes here. And they say he has God's curse on him, with which the old woman cursed him ten years ago when he bade the sergeants distrain."

"All that is news to me," said Boutroux, holding her in the darkness, "and whatever news you have is as pleasant as the noise of a brook. But I learn nothing of my fate."

"He did but salute me then," she continued in her whispered, halting anxiety, "but when an hour later I left you, having given you food in that brief moment, he was waiting with my companions at the well; and he said, 'Joïse' (which is their nickname for my name Joyeuse; and that is a nickname, for my true name is Isabel)—'Joïse, there are men in this country looking for coin.'"

"That is a thing, my dear," said Boutroux gently, "that twenty men to my own knowledge have looked for in their time, and only one or two now and then have found it."

"Oh, let me tell you," she said, and sighed. "He said to me threateningly, 'They are looking for coin.' 'For what coin?' said I, roughly. It is he who comes with a set wooing every Sunday eve before the Mass and on the eve of the feast days to sit by the fire; and he claims to sit next me, and my father will have it so. Since it is so, I must treat him lovingly or roughly;

I treat him roughly, for I will treat him in no other way."

"You do well," said Boutroux, "to treat all men roughly; they are rough, and rough treatment is in the nature of roughness. Friend, rough on!"

"Friend," she said, "when he spoke about that coin I knew what he meant. He meant the money paid you for the sack of charcoal."

"And why? . . . And if they do? . . . It was not marked," said Boutroux; "and even if it were marked, I have it here, and I can bury it—none can know of that sack or of me, save you only."

"Friend," she said, "listen. The charcoal-burners say, and have said it to the Justice, that they had been robbed of their charcoal. They missed but that one sack; of that they complain less. But they complain most about a purse in which they kept their common earnings, and of a fine roll of cloth which one of them had bought at the Fair. They will have it that a wandering man deprived them of these things. One says that he has seen him."

"Then he lies," said Boutroux; "and that wandering man took nothing but the charcoal sack, and took it at a great risk, which paid for it. No—wait—he did also take good wine and doubtful bread. I remember his taking it, for it was I. But as for the purse, he never heard of it ; and for the roll of cloth, he would as soon steal a beech tree or a wolf trap to burden him upon his going."

"Then," she went on still fevered, "in the village one and another complains to the Justice during the day that they have lost this or that ; and, friend, in a word, they are hunting for a man."

"See how a hunter can be hunted ! " said Boutroux. "It is a double world."

"I would have you out by night," she said, "here and now, although your going would leave me so that after these few hours all the rest of my life would be ringing like a steeple at a dying, with nothing else but the dying of these few hours. But I cannot have it so, because there is another thing."

"And what is that ? "

"If I tell you, you will be angry," she answered, and was silent ; and though he questioned her and pressed her, she would tell him nothing at all, nor speak to him for a little while. Then she said,—

"In the great city there was some one who

killed a man, and he did it against The People. They say that they have traced him to our woods, and the Commune has been advised by the Commune of the city, and the Commune of the city has sent armed men. Now, though you should go by night, they know you, friend (for you I think it was that killed the man); you would not traverse this country, which is unknown to you, at the first dawning, without falling into some village without disguise, and you would be caught and held."

"It was I," said Boutroux, "who killed the man."

He felt the form that he held shrink at those few words, and for a moment something lifted in his mind, letting in a light, as it were, upon his reason, and making him afraid of his own self. He heard again the first engagement of steel, and it seemed to him in a sort of lightning vision something so evil that he would have no more to do with it than with venom or with treason. He smelt sulphur in the sparks of the steel; but, as rapid as the flash of those sparks in his memory, the impression faded, and he was back in his old security.

"I fought," said he a little sullenly. "If it had been *he* that had had the better of *me*, my ghost would never have complained — least of all to a woman."

"Friend," she said softly, "I am not blaming you."

"Did they tell you more?" he added; "did they speak of a house or of friends? Or did they give you any name or description?"

"No," she said in a bold whisper, and lied; for in the gossip and the offered reward, in the speech of his pursuers, and from his own manner, she had easily made out the truth, and she knew him for what he was: his name, his house, and all his story.

"I am tired to hear so much of these perils," he said to her in another tone. "I can see, through the door of this open prison, that the moon is up. I dare not go out with you, for you tell me that everything is watched, and yet you tell me also that this place cannot be suspected."

She grasped his wrists with her hands, and he wondered at their sudden strength in the darkness.

"Oh," she said, "try no more adventures, but wait until I show you a way; for in that moonlight, if they should see from any window any form coming hence it would go very ill;

and if they should see two together, two would suffer, friend, for how would my people bear to see me with a stranger?"

"I will not go out," he said. . . . "How clear are these nights, from the midnight onward, when the moon has risen!"

"You shall stay here," she said, "and I will come always at night-fall, and I will be with you all the unknown hours, and leave you a little before the dawning, and there shall be our farewells. For in a little time, when seven days have passed, and we have the dark of the moon, and I have found some tale to tell, and some wrong scent to put them on, then, oh my friend, you will go out, and I will go with you. But I shall not follow you beyond some place of safety, which I shall have prepared."

"If I so desire," he said, "you will follow me."

She answered nothing at all. For all that night, until just before the dawning, they were together in the hiding-place.

CHAPTER X.

In which Two Lovers find themselves in the Daylight.

SO one day passed, and another, and twice in every daylight she brought him food ; and after the fall of night he would sometimes creep out a little and breathe the air and look furtively from the shadow of the low wooden wall at the lights in the houses far off, and wait until, when all those lights were darkened, before the rising of the moon, she would come to him where he awaited her. And it seemed to him during those days as though many years were passing, and it seemed to him also as though two lives had been appointed for him—one the life before he knew such vigils, but the other the life after them.

Never in all those long secret companionships did he hear her voice aloud, nor she his ; nor did they dare go out alone together beyond the walls of his hiding-place or breathe the air outside, until, upon the evening of the seventh day, while the lights were still shining in the windows, and long before he had expected her, he heard footsteps, not at the door, but behind the hut, and through the chinks of it a voice that called him gently, not by any name, but calling him friend.

"You must rise," she said, "friend, if you are sleeping; and if you are not sleeping you must rise. You must come crouching round swiftly to the back here where I am and where is a deep shadow, and then we will go together to a place I know."

Even as she spoke in whispers, those whispers were so lamentable that his heart broke for her. And when he came to her in that shadow, he said, "What does it matter to me, Joyeuse, whether I escape or no?"

"Ah," said she, "friend, shall we be longer one with the other if they make you a prisoner? I think not! You are caught every way if you remain; and if you do what I shall tell you, though we never see each other any more, you shall be free; and if you are free it is with God and His holy ones whether we meet again." When she had said this she went quickly before him along the darkness of the hedge towards the brook and the line of the woodland, and he

followed.   Then she went by a path she knew
into the underwood, and he still went after.

As they went the last sounds of the village were
lost behind them, and sleep came upon it and upon
the wild wood ; and as it was the dark of the moon,
they went secure from men.   Twice he called to
her, and twice he would have halted ; but she
answered only by commands and still went forward,
until they came after many hours to an open place
in the wild wood.   Here there was a pond, and
near the pond a lonely farmhouse, quite dumb and
sleeping and silent.   But the dogs heard them and
barked, and Joyeuse was afraid.

"Come quickly with me," she said ; "we are
not yet at the end.   There is a place of safety for
you beyond."

The wood closed upon them again beyond the
clearing ; she still led forward.   It seemed at last
that the branches against the sky were somewhat
more clearly marked, and again they came to a
standing water.   Boutroux thought that it looked
paler and deader than does water in the dim of the
night, and more staring.   And then in a few
moments more it was evidently day, though but
the beginning of the day ; and with that light it
came upon him that he was not fit to be in such
company, and that all that business with her which

go away. I have a place of safety for you and a plan."

As she said this the beauty of her young eyes filled with tears, and she watched him in a manner which he suddenly remembered he had seen in the face of his mother when she had watched him as a little child. And once again Boutroux within the depths of his heart marvelled at the complexity of this world.

"Of all things," he thought to himself, "I should have imagined that at least they cared for shaving. But there are three things no man can quite understand, and one of them I have always heard is horses, and the other is the sea, and it would seem that the third is Joyeuse."

They had left their seat and they had come to the great royal road. But without proceeding along it Joyeuse led him straight to a cottage by its side, at the door of which a woman, neat—too neat—severe, aged, and expectant, changed from an expression of suspicion at their coming to an expression somewhat more genial as she saw the girl and knew her again.

"Well, Joïse," she said—"or since you are now so old, shall I call you Isabel?" She looked with a mixture of disapproval and of command upon Boutroux's wretched externals, but he was holding himself very well, and there was a gallant strength about his going with which she should not have been displeased. "Sir," she said in a formal manner, "since you have suffered for the King—and I have heard the whole story from my foster-child—you may claim from me anything you will."

"I claim nothing," he said.

"You shall have your life at any rate," said the old woman. She said it in the peasants' manner, and Boutroux heard in her tone the false kindness of peasants bargaining. He looked full in her hard eyes and wondered what the price of his safety would be—and whether he would choose to pay it.

The old woman, standing before the pair of them at her threshold in the cool morning, was making a plan. She said,—

"Come into my house, sir, for the roads are not always safe these times for every one, even though the sun be not yet risen."

The girl was not asked, but she followed. Boutroux, as he passed that cottage door, felt a separation and a changing. He felt a plot in the place. Better be flying and hiding, he thought, and no one's will but my own to guide me, than be subject to the calculations of others—and the interest of this Hag of the Years.

He watched the old woman leave the room on her errand for him. Her very walk seemed too secret and determined; he mistrusted her absence as he mistrusted her presence.

"Joyeuse," he said, "what is this old woman into whose hands you have delivered me?"

"Her name is Perrin," said Joyeuse: her lovely eyes were more anxious than her lover's; she looked at him and pleaded, divining his suspicion and his fears.

"What is her plan with me?" he asked.

"I cannot tell—I dare not know. . . . Before her substance grew, in old days, when my mother died, my father hired her to his farm, and she fostered me. In her second marriage she came to this place. Oh! do as she bids you. She has power in this countryside."

"Joyeuse," he whispered, with his laughing eyes full upon her, "how did you speak of me to her? What have I suffered for the King? For God's sake brief me in the lie."

"You got the wound from some Jacobin," she said, "and you are a fugitive. And, friend," she added, putting her mouth close to his ear, "I thought I would give you some name or other; but I did not. I thought of saying that your name was Boutroux."

"Lie for lie, Joyeuse," said Boutroux; "and since you love them so much, let me tell you, upon my side, a little lie of my own. I will say I was in a hut hidden for some days, but much more especially for some nights, by a woman from a hamlet the name of which I do not know. But she had three names—Joïse for her betrothed, and for her father Isabel, but for me Joyeuse. Then we went through a wood together, and the day dawned. When the day dawned I understood why I had dreamed of her beauty."

"The one tale may be as false as the other," said Joyeuse.

They were standing in the bare, clean kitchen of that place. The old woman had not yet come back from her errand; they still faced each other, alone.

"Joyeuse," he said, "when I went to school I heard a fairy tale, and I will tell it you now, that you may always remember it."

"Tell on," she said.

"Joyeuse," he said, "the fairy tale was this: That once there was the daughter of a king whom Love himself made love to. And they were to watch together all night until the dawn, and they were to possess each other for ever;

but upon this condition, that she should never see his face. Joyeuse, it so happened that she saw his face, and then she lost him for good and all."

"She would not so have lost him had he kept about him some charm," answered the girl slowly. "Have you no charm?"

"I have," said he, "as you should know. It is a gold medal of Rocamadour which my mother gave me when I was a child. I have it on the chain at my neck, a silver chain, and till I lose it no great harm will befall my body. . . ."

As he said this the old woman returned, and said to him,—

"Follow me. In what I have planned for you you must be dressed in a certain fashion, and you must clean yourself and be shaven. There is a plan laid for you whereby you shall be safe."

"In what you have planned for me!" he muttered, wondering, as he followed her. "In what you have planned . . ."

He followed her into a little room, where were soap and a razor and water prepared. There was a suit of good woollen cloth upon the bed, which suit was in the fashion of those hills: a young farmer's Sunday suit, or one for feast-days. There was a rough shirt to go with it, and a pair of laced shoes well greased; and Boutroux with all these made himself once more a man, but this time a peasant of substance.

A small square of looking-glass, unframed, hung from a nail. There were black patches on it, due to age, but in it he saw that the disgrace of his hiding had disappeared. He felt less free. It was not his own disguise. He felt himself a comedian at another's bidding, and he loathed and dreaded the change. He was like a man who is led blindfold with a strong hand upon his wrist, and led, perhaps, on purposes not his own. Moreover, the sleeplessness of the night fell upon him, and he suddenly felt fatigued.

He came back to the little low kitchen with that fatigue apparent upon him, and eager for the refreshment of her face. . . . The room was stark bare. Its emptiness of her struck him like a chill of presentiment. There was no one there, only the old peasant woman, standing strict and forbidding, who watched him hardly; she was ready with orders rather than with counsel. She so eyed him, waiting for him to speak.

" Madame," he said, "where is that foster-daughter of yours with whom I came?"

"She has gone out, I think," said the peasant woman steadily; "but it is no matter, for your business now is with my son."

"Madame," said Boutroux courteously, "you are invaluable to me! And, pray, what else do you command? My purse is at your service . . . true, it is empty. Or would you rather that I should forswear myself, or perhaps steal or kill to your advantage? What have you told Joyeuse?" he added suddenly, in a more brutal voice. "Where have you sent her?"

"Sir," said the old woman as steadily as ever, "I may tell you that I respect any man who has been wounded in the right cause, and I know that you were wounded. I know by whom—and I know whom you wounded also —and where."

"Oh, Madame," said Boutroux elaborately, "you have the advantage of me! . . . you have hold of some romance that is new to me. Nay, it is indifferent to me—profoundly. But where is Joyeuse?"

"Young man, you understand me clearly," continued the peasant woman, with fixed thin lips, "and you will understand me further. Nothing is given for nothing. If you will lose your head, lose it. If you would end safe, you will obey and be tame. Climb up into the cart that is now at my door and sit beside my son, who is to drive it. Go where he shall drive you, and accept what I choose to offer you. It is not a pastime, nor what you might have chosen. . . . But it is pleasanter than a short imprisonment and a public death."

"Where is Joyeuse, old hag?" said Boutroux again. "You will excuse me, Madame, if my words touch upon the picturesque; but I think I have been tricked in some way."

The old lady was quite unmoved. "I am bound to tell you nothing, young man," she said. "I offer you safety, and you reply in a way that gives me a good right to do with you what I choose. She is not here. Do you know what is here, within call? Ten of my men in a barn, my son, whom you can hear calling from his cart, and there are arms. There is something else. There are, round the turning of the road, still sleeping in the inn, officers of the police from Bordeaux. Do you understand me?"

"Old woman," said Boutroux insolently, and swaggering up a little towards her, "you have heard the saying that one may as well be hanged for a sheep as for a lamb; and I take it that of the two you are less a lamb than a sheep. You have heard it said that I killed a man?"

"Yes," said the old woman; "and I believe it." She did not shrink from him; she fixed her small eyes on him like needle points.

"And if Joyeuse was where those armed men are with their writs and their warrants, do you think"—and he came a step nearer—"that, to see her again for a moment or two, I would hesitate to put another item into the indictment?"

As he so spoke he stepped back suddenly. A man had lumbered in through the doorway, and stood at his shoulder.

"You're quarrelling with mother," he grinned. "They mainly do . . . but she beats un. Don't 'ee, Dame?"

The mother said nothing; for the first time that morning she smiled, and it was a drawn smile.

"I were to give 'ee this," went on the yokel, "and to tell 'ee . . ." He grinned again.

As the young man said this he showed Boutroux in the midst of his enormous palm a very small medal lying; and Boutroux, rapidly and instinctively feeling through his shirt at his chest, found the chain there alone and no medal attached to it. He picked the medal gently from that big hand: it was his medal right enough; it was his medal of gold. On the one side was the figure, on the other the legend. He hoicked out from his bosom the end of the chain, as though he would fasten the charm on again; then, thinking better of it, he put the chain back in his bosom and the medal in his pocket. He asked himself in what moment the lover's theft was done, and he thought he remembered; and as he so remembered, he smiled.

"You should have kept it for proof and a clue when you betray me," he said.

"You are a mad fool," answered the old lady. "You have done harm enough in the place. If I had kept your medal I would have kept it for the gold. There's no clue wanted for a face like yours. If my son did not need you to feed the rebels in his place, I had rather the hangman had you. . . . But you are to go to the armies, and go you will. It falls well for us. Go and sell your flesh."

The sun had risen. He must go, or find himself a prisoner. He considered the chances of life and a possible vengeance. He decided, and followed the young farmer out to the cart that waited.

"You are right, Madame," said he over his shoulder; "I am a fool, and passably mad. And you, Madame, are an accursed old Royalist witch whom my honest friends the Jacobins will do well to burn. I will send them, never fear, and you and your house above you and your damned traitor serfs will be roasted and pass in smoke."

The old lady did not fail.

"Go and replace my son: you are fitter meat for Brunswick," she called after him. "We have a use for your carrion."

"But I have no use for you," shouted Boutroux from the road. "Go and join your father the devil—my friends shall send you there."

He climbed up into the cart. The big peasant, overjoyed at the completion of the business, gave a little click with his tongue and a flick with his whip; the horse jerked, pulled itself into a slow trot, and they lumbered heavily up the road.

CHAPTER XI.

Showing how Men become Soldiers.

THE road was hollow and rising on a sharp incline, paved as a royal road should be, and wide.

In a matter of half a mile they came to the summit of the hill; here was a turn and a clump of wood which, when they had passed it, hid from Boutroux the hut and all his memories.

Before them from that height was to be seen under the newly-risen sun a broad and excellent champaign, woodlands and vineyards, a wide river running through, which surely, he thought, must be a stretch of the Dordogne. Far beyond, framing this delightful prospect and hazy against the sky, stood noble and exalted distant hills. With all that sight the thought of what he had lost was mingled. The peasant had halted his lumbering great horse and his rough cart: he was waiting for some appointment.

"Why do you not go on?" said Boutroux.

"Maybe I've a friend," said the other young man, grinning his broadest. "We've all a right to our appointments."

Boutroux constrained himself, and within his mind did no more than to add, by way of codicil, a special curse upon the son, to follow that good larger curse which he had laid upon his mother and her home. But even as this passed through his imaginings he saw standing by the step of the cart a labouring man, old, grizzled, and thin, who saluted them in a clumsy fashion and climbed up on to the board at the back of the cart behind them. With the fall of the road the horse was urged to a sharp trot. Boutroux was ill content.

"Who is that man?" he asked.

"One o' the hands," said his companion, with no further explanation.

"Do you need him?"

"I hopes not! . . . But 'tis allas useful to find another along wi' un."

The cart halted to take a piece of rise at a walk, and as it halted the old labourer behind slid to the ground and walked behind it, like one watching and guarding.

Boutroux leaped down from the cart and came close up to the old man, who recoiled much more than that woman in the hut had done. He said to him,—

"I shall track you, and I shall follow you : you shall pay the price for this plot, whatever it is. . . . Where am I being taken to ?"

The old man winced and still backed away ; he would not answer ; he half cowered.

"Doan you be a fool," said the driver, looking back at the scene as he halted. "Come up 'long-side me."

"Old man," said Boutroux, as he got up into the cart again, "it will be ill for you at the end of this journey, and worse for you later on. Be wise and go home." But the old man clambered on again to his back-board ; Boutroux said no more. The road fell again in a straight fall of a mile and more before them, and he sat silently beside the yokel mile after mile.

Once in that long stretch of downward road he pulled the medal from his pocket and looked at it. He put it back. At last, after a long and rustic silence, he again asked the fellow at his side where he was being driven, and what was all this plan.

The peasant looked at him with sidelong eyes and smirked to himself, whipped up the horse (which shambled not much the faster for it), then

looked again with another such glance, and said :
"What might your name be?"

A false name was on the tip of Boutroux's
tongue, but he was too angry for prudence. He
said : "It's none of your business what my name
may be!"

"My business more 'n most," chuckled the
rustic, "my business more 'n most, seeing your
name's to be my name in an hour or so, and
mine yours. . . . *My* name is Perrin."

"How is your name to be my name?" said
Boutroux, falling with an ease that surprised him
into that conversation of parables and hints which
is the very expression of a peasantry.

His companion nudged him suddenly and unpleasantly in the ribs. "Who goes a-soldiering?"
he said, and winked.

"God knows!" said Boutroux : but he put
this with what the old cat had said of selling his
flesh to the rebels, and he began to understand.

The cart was half-way down the long slow
descent, the glory of the landscape had diminished,
the distant hills were masked by nearer folds of
land ; the day, now that the sun had risen, began
even thus early to show signs of heat ; a sort of
sleepiness was on him mixed with ill-temper, and
for a good ten minutes he said nothing more, but

he was determined to know what was before him. He could not bear to resign his freedom to the army, yet he knew that he would have to do so lest a worse constraint should fall upon him.

Just as he had determined to speak again he saw far down the road before them three mounted men in uniform. As the cart approached them, he made out a sergeant, old and grizzled, and with him two quite young men of some cavalry regiment with whose facings he was unfamiliar, and which he could not name.

Boutroux and his driver came up to that small patrol, and even as they reached it the peasant, sitting at Boutroux's right, put up a hand as though warning the sergeant to make no sign. He beckoned to the soldier, got him to his side, and began whispering to him in the confidential way of peasants ; when the whispering was over the soldier looked up doubtfully into Boutroux's face, and Boutroux looked ironically into his.

" Perrin ? " he said.

Boutroux winked slightly, and was silent.

" Perrin is your name ? " said the soldier again, asking the question in full.

" Very possibly," said Boutroux. " It is a matter upon which I should wish to know more before I committed myself."

The old sergeant smiled grimly. "You are not the only one," said he, "who in these days must be decently careful. Come, I will not bother you as to whether your name is Perrin. What the regiment needs, my lad, is a Perrin's two legs and two arms and some sort of a head, the duller the better. Have you a dull head, Perrin?"

"Oh yes," said Boutroux, "my head is dull enough for the Militia, or for the Ministry of War."

"You can't shirk," said the sergeant; "and the less you answer the better."

"I don't want to shirk," said Boutroux, "but I do want to thresh out that question of my name. Note you, Sergeant, a name is an important thing: not in itself but in the repetition of it; for if a man's name goes on changing like a marquis's son's, it is a disturbance to all the world."

"Oh, give yourself any name you like, lad, only get down and follow."

"How far?"

"Why," said the sergeant, with a laugh that was hoarse with the life he had led, "my orders are as far as Angoulême . . . but the enemy are nearer the Rhine."

"Angoulême?" said Boutroux, fixing his eyes upon a distant tree. " . . . That's lucky . . ."

He sighed. "That's one of the luckiest things I've ever heard. In Angoulême, Sergeant, it so precisely happens, there lives the only man in all this country who may know my name. I shall forget it myself until I find him."

"There are many like you," muttered the sergeant; and Boutroux climbed down from the cart and stood by the side of the soldier's horse.

"Now, you will follow quietly?" said the grey old fellow, looking down.

"Not if you trot," said Boutroux carelessly. "No man can follow a trotting horse quietly."

"We'll mount you in the town," said the sergeant; and as he said it the rustic, immensely relieved, turned his cart round, gave them all the blessing of God, and was for returning in peace to his home. But Boutroux, as he turned, spoke a word to the sergeant, and said,—

"Sergeant, I am a man of honour."

"They all say that," said the sergeant suspiciously.

"Not only am I a man of honour, Sergeant, but you are mounted and we are in the midst of open fields, where there is no cover for a hunted man. Come, let me say a word privately to the driver of this cart : to tell you the truth, I have a message for my friend—from the Jacobins."

The sergeant did not answer, but he did nothing to prevent the movement. He was used to such scenes in the pressing of men. Boutroux strolled up to the driver just as that rustic was trying to get some pace out of his old jade; he came up by his side and said,—

"Halt a minute!"

The yokel pulled up, cursing.

"We must make an arrangement—for both our sakes. I think you said my name was Perrin, did you not?"

"That's what I said," answered the youth, and grinned.

"I think you said that your name was my name?"

"That's it," said the peasant, and grinned more broadly.

"Very well, Perrin," said Boutroux—and he said "Very well" with a decision that unpleasantly reminded the peasant of his lord. "Very well, Perrin, listen! Your crops this year will fail you: you will not pay your taxes. The men-at-arms will come to distrain upon your filthy hovel, but before they take your sticks the men of my society will find you; they will bind and beat that old hag of a mother of yours;"—the peasant did not dare to strike him—"and when they have done so, a worse thing will happen to you all. They will sack your place, they will kill you as they choose, and you perhaps will be burned upon the wood of your own woodpile. They have more power than you know."

"Oh, we care nothing for prophecies in my village," said the rustic, a little pale. "Go your way; you are a soldier man now: better for you than for me!"

"I only wanted you to look forward to it," said Boutroux, "because it will make you suffer more until the time shall come. Meanwhile . . . " He leapt suddenly on to the step of the cart, threw the old labourer to the ground, half stunning him, and in the same moment struck the driver with his fist full drive in the mouth.

Blood poured from it; the victim of the blow beat the air with his hands, and roared for an arrest. He had clambered down, the blood still streaming from his broken teeth—he was mumbling and cursing for an arrest; the old labourer had picked himself up and was tearing away down the road. The sergeant would offer no redress.

"Yours to catch the birds," he said, "and theirs to curse you. The hussars are not your policemen! get you home!"

The fellow limped painfully to his seat; he

moved off promising pursuit, and Boutroux turned back to the sergeant's side.

"I have given my message," he said, "and now we can all go forward."

The two privates were laughing. They were used to the impotent anger of pressed men, and they liked to see them game. They drew up their horses behind him, and Boutroux walked beside the sergeant's bridle, now and then exchanging a word, the sergeant at one remark of his or another smiling down under his grey old moustaches, amused at such a recruit, until they came to the gate of a little walled town, and there a guard was standing.

The old sergeant dismounted stiffly, and Boutroux most politely held his bridle; but the sergeant turned his horse to one of the two men, and beckoned Boutroux into the guard-room.

There was a rough table in it with pen and ink, and a dirty fold of paper upon which was printed the regimental arms and the King's regulations. The sergeant summoned two witnesses and ran through the formula of the oath. When he came to the recruit's name he muttered aside to Boutroux : "Come, you must give a name—any name."

"But," said Boutroux calmly, "how am I to know my name until I get to Angoulême?"

"I must fill in something," said the sergeant fiercely.

"I would give the name of Perrin," said Boutroux thoughtfully, "were it not so unlucky! Such damnable things are to happen to a gentleman of that family!"

"Put down Perrin," said the sergeant; and Boutroux signed "G. B. Perrin" in a sharp and educated hand, with a rapidity of the pen that was suspicious; but in those days of August and the invasion, questions were not too closely pressed.

"Perrin," said the sergeant, finishing the formula, "you do here swear on your conscience, and with this oath, to the Nation, that you will loyally and duly, etc., etc. . . . and that's all over!"

"Is that the oath?" said Perrin.

"Yes," said the sergeant, beginning to show signs of sharpness. "We've done with joking now, my boy."

"Well, then, there it is; and what's the new way of swearing?"

The sergeant looked up puzzled. "I forget," he said. "There used to be God in it, eh?"

A man of the guards said respectfully: "They

swear with the right hand spread outward now, Sergeant."

"Do they?" said the old sergeant surlily. He was a Tory.

Boutroux spread out his right hand. The sergeant put his hand in the pocket of his leather breeches for a coin, and found none there. "We must have the coin," he said stupidly. "It's in the essence of the contract."

"And what is the least coin necessary?" said Boutroux.

"One livre," said the sergeant; "it's the law, and has been ever since I first knew the service, God curse it!"

"Why, then," said Boutroux genially, "let me lend you the coin." He pulled out a handful of silver and put down the franc.

The sergeant took it and pushed it back across the table towards him; in so doing, he spoke the last words of the ritual, "And as you take this coin, so you are engaged."

"Precisely," said Boutroux.

The sergeant picked the franc up, rang it to test its value, and quietly slipped it into his own breeches pocket. "It is a custom of the regiment," he said. "We do not return the earnest money."

"Naturally," said Boutroux, "naturally. But have you spat upon it for luck?"

"You have shown more money than is good for you," was the sergeant's only answer. "You'll have to stand wine." He handed the coin to one of the guard, Boutroux reluctantly added two more, and the man came back with some very good wine of Chardac, little enough for three whole livres of silver—but soldiers are always cheated. They drank together to the new recruit.

"It is against the King's regulations," said the sergeant stiffly, "for superiors to drink with inferiors! Hum! Therefore, Private Perrin, you will drink first and I after, and in that way we shall not drink together! . . . Has any one a little gunpowder?" he added more genially.

The private soldier standing by shook his head. "We are allowed no service cartridges," he said.

"I thought as much," said the sergeant thoughtfully; "we shall have to make it up in snuff." He took a pinch from a box which he had about him and carefully peppered Boutroux's wine therewith. "Now, my boy," he said kindly, "drink that; it will make a man of you."

Boutroux drank the wine.

"It is this kind of wine," said the private

soldier sententiously, "that makes a man sneeze, not in his nose but in his stomach."

"It is good wine," said Boutroux, "but the snuff seemed somehow to spoil it. How does it taste without snuff, Sergeant?"

"It is better," said the sergeant, smacking his lips and speaking slowly—"it is better without snuff."

"Why, then," said Perrin, "pour me some out unseasoned."

This they did; and when Perrin had drunk it, the sergeant looking at him gravely the while, that old soldier said,—

"Perrin, my poor lad, let me give you some advice, and if you take it you will be a wise man. In the service we love boldness and sauce, but we treat them hardly; and if they go too far we treat them ill."

"Sergeant," said Perrin, with deference, "it was the snuff that went to my head; by now I am quite cured."

"Take him away," said the old chap. As he said it, he sat down to fill up certain papers, establishing the new recruit in his corps; and Boutroux was led away by two of his new companions, looking and feeling odd between them in his civilian dress.

As they went, one of them said, " What roped you in ?"

" Debt," answered Boutroux promptly.

" Ah!" said his guard, sighing, "and no wonder!" He knew that gate of entry into the service.

" Yes," said Boutroux, "debt. I cut a man's coat with a long knife, and the damages were more than I could pay. But the Perrins are an unlucky family, and there's worse coming on those who stayed behind."

They said nothing more to him for a hundred yards or so ; but as they approached the town hall of the place, one of them, nodding towards it, said, "There's a pack of others like you in there!"

Boutroux did not answer. They led him into a great basement hall vaulted in stone, and there he found a score or so of every kind and condition : young volunteers from the place, two or three gentlemen's sons, a fellow plainly out of jail who later boasted of it, and one, a Basque, who had come northward leading a bear and who could not make out what in the world had happened to him, but who, with all these others, had been caught and was to be made into a soldier.

Overlooking this crowd was a young, mild-eyed man, in the same uniform of the cavalry as had been worn by Boutroux's first captors. The stripes upon his arm were of cloth and not of gold ; he was apparently inferior in some way, but he seemed to have a command.

His voice was gentle, low, and deep, and he was kind to them all. He formed them in that basement hall into a sort of rough column with a front of four ; and when he had them so formed he looked anxiously at the little squad, and said mildly, like a man asking the time of day or passing some remark upon the weather, " March ! " Having so said, he went out of that hall, through the great door, into the garden of the town hall, and the little column shambled after him.

"There is a lack of parade about all this," thought Boutroux.

In the garden they found a person of great splendour, a little effeminate in speech, well clothed and beautifully armed.

"And this," said Boutroux to himself, "is an officer ! "

This being gave orders to the young soldier who had marched them into the garden, and the lot of them were led away to a barn where deep and clean straw was laid. The young soldier who had brought them spoke again in his mild, monotonous voice, as though he were repeating a lesson,—

"Those of you who wish to sleep, may sleep; any who desire to go into the town may do so. But it is forbidden to send any letter or to approach the postmaster or his stables. At noon I will come for those who can ride; the others will remain here. Arrange it among yourselves."

He left them, and the dispirited band began discussing which of them could ride. Two opinions arose in their debate: one was that all of them could ride, the other that none could ride. For there were some who thought that those who could not ride would be discharged; but there were others who thought that, on the contrary, all would be kept, and those who could ride would have a better and earlier chance of easy treatment. In the end, it was decided to decide nothing. One boy who wept continually and asserted that horses terrified him, was marked out as a butt by his fellows.

"If they desire," said a large, bold young man, whose trade it had been to sell cheese, "some one of us who certainly cannot ride, we will hand over this friend," and he pointed to the weeping figure. When he had so spoken they disposed

themselves upon the straw. Those who, like
Boutroux, had had no repose during the whole
night (and they were many), fell at once into a
deep and exhausted sleep : the remainder talked,
some despairingly, some eagerly, one with another ;
not a few were curious and pleased to find themselves upon the edge of soldiering. The little
man who had cried wandered about by himself ;
if he had dared, he would have run away, but
he had no friends and he did not know the
country.

Boutroux, being of those who slept, saw nothing
of this. What woke him at noon was the tearing
noise of a trumpet in the very door of the barn ;
and as he sat up in the straw, exhausted and
bewildered, he saw before him again that mild
young man in uniform and sword, who tapped
him on the shoulder and said,—

"Come ! I cannot afford to have any one
late !"

In a field outside the barn there were twenty
horses of every sort and kind, most of them old,
all of them unenthusiastic, waiting saddled with
the heavy campaign saddle of the service. The
young uniformed man, as gently as ever, put
a man to each horse, and then said dolefully,
"Mount." Those of the twenty who did not

know how this was done were taken away: some punishment was in store for them. Of the ten who at least could mount, eight wished they had not, as did their horses too. And of these eight, six were told in that same quiet voice to come off again, and went to join their unfortunate companions. Of the remaining four was Boutroux. The young, quiet man went up to Boutroux and said,—

"Look here, my friend, it will save time and trouble if you will tell me frankly, since there are only four of you, do you or do you not ride?"

"I can ride this beast," said Boutroux. "As for the other three, you can find out by touching up their mounts with any stick that comes handy; and mind you, when I say I can ride this brute, I only judge by his ears, which seem to be made of soft cloth."

The young soldier smiled a gentle smile. "Yes," he said, sighing, "I ought to have put you upon a more vicious beast; but our mounts are worn. Have you ridden?"

"Oh yes," said Boutroux, "I have ridden." He was on the point of saying, "I was a postilion for a night," but he checked himself.

"It is a pity," sighed the young man; "we can

never make a good hussar out of a man who has ridden as a civilian."

The four were trotted round and round. Three could sit their beasts, Boutroux among them. One fell off at the first sign of motion ; he was dismissed into an outer darkness, and the young soldier, left with the three, said : "That decides it ; three out of ten ! "

He went back to make his report. The three found themselves set apart in the stables, sweeping up, cleaning and baiting, and later carrying pails of water. As they did so the young soldier gently reminded them that these advantages they owed to their power over the brute creation.

"We make three classes of recruits," he said : "some must march behind, to be drilled and catch us up as they can ; others we can mount, and they ride with us to where we join and are drilled on the march ; others we incorporate if they can ride at all. Such are the times we live in, and they are evil. Of the twenty who were netted here, ten said they rode ; of these you three can for your sins remain seated with difficulty upon a jaded horse—on which account," he added, sighing again, "there is attributed to you the very noble service of stable duty." He appointed a sort of bully from among the older soldiers to look after them, and went off to take his orders.

At five o'clock the three found themselves mounted, with the young, sad soldier by their side, following at the tail of a long train of cavalry that was filing out of the town. As they passed the further gate the trumpets sounded again in a grand and challenging manner.

"It is a wonderful thing," said Boutroux to the sad young soldier, "but these trumpets do not frighten my horse at all."

"The inferior," answered the young soldier politely, quoting as from a book—"the inferior does not address his superior until his superior has addressed him."

"I'm sure I'm very sorry," said Boutroux.

"Had you been longer in the service," said the young soldier quietly, by way of answer, "I would for that last remark have reported you for punishment."

This said, they rode side by side for some two miles in complete silence.

The road went on monotonous and meaningless, and Boutroux thought as he went that the life of a soldier was something quite utterly different from anything that he had conceived. Then he got a new light upon it.

Far off a voice gave a loud, long-drawn cry that sounded like no word he had ever heard, and at once right down the line there passed a sort of wave of trotting. It reached him and his two companions, and the young soldier who looked after them. They also broke into a shambling trot. He had heard that a soldier must not rise in his stirrups, and as he was wondering what alternative a soldier had, he was surprised to find his leader turn to him and say,—

"Now that we are trotting and there is a noise, we can talk."

"I'm delighted to hear you say so," Boutroux gasped between the jolts of the saddle. "Did you notice the poor child among us who was crying?"

"Oh yes," said the young soldier, with even more than his accustomed sadness.

"Has he found the service too hard in these few hours?" asked Boutroux pitifully.

"No," said the young soldier, musing; "he was not capable of anything, so we made him a servant to the captain of Troop B. The captain's wife thought he would make a good servant . . . he will have an easy time. Better for him than for us!"

"And will he make a good servant?" said Boutroux.

"No," said the other, "but he will not have to ride now or at any other time. And, oh Lord! he will get more money than we do."

CHAPTER XII.

Showing how Soldiers are not always so.

IT was two days later when the trumpet sounded before dawn in the streets of a straggling village, and the men woke grumbling from the straw in the barns and took their horses from the stables to saddle them, and mustered at last in the market square.

The march was to be a short one : they were within eight miles of Angoulême.

The odd procession with its civilians and its uniformed troops, its veterans, its young recruits as yet undrilled, moved out along the great highway. They had not gone a mile in that summer morning when there came up at a gallop a man on horseback from far away down the road. He rode as men ride in action, and as though he bore news of immediate consequence. He was an orderly. He spoke to the head of the detachment, saluting, and he handed him the paper that he bore. The officer read the paper, looked puzzled, and exchanged some words with the orderly; then bade him go down the column and explain in detail to the non-commissioned officers, especially to the *fourriers*. That orderly came down the column to where the gentle-faced young man rode, as was his place, by Boutroux's side at the tail of the line. The orderly had something smart about him as of the old service, before the Revolution and the invasion, but he was very tired. He was sitting his horse anyhow, as though he had ridden too long, and the first thing that the gentle-faced young man said to him was, "Who shortened your stirrups?" He said it familiarly, for they were of equal rank.

"It is your eyes that deceive you, Hamard," said the other, mocking him; "no man in the hussars ever shortens his stirrups. I opportunely changed the length of my legs by quite six inches a mile up the road. You must see that my legs are beyond the regulation length."

"That explains it," said the other gravely, and Boutroux wondered whether this were the wit of the regiment, "for if so," thought he, "I must prepare myself to make jests of the kind."

"What have you there, Hamard?" said the newcomer, jerking with his chin at Boutroux as he sat in his peasant clothes upon the horse.

"Why," said the sad-faced young sergeant whose name Boutroux thus heard, "that object explains itself."

"It does," said the newcomer. "Are you quite sure of him?"

"We're not sure of anybody," said Sergeant Hamard. "You, for instance. How did you leave things in Angoulême?"

"There were," said the messenger, looking at the sky as though he would find his words there; "there were *two* officers left with the regiment when it reached Angoulême—a captain and a lieutenant. The others had preferred to serve the enemy; they had gone away."

"Two, that's short rations! Two, and not a major among them!"

"No," said the messenger slowly, "nor a captain now. He is no longer there."

"No wonder," said the young sergeant; "the service is a hole from which a man will escape if he can."

"True," said the other; "the lieutenant, however, after some hesitation, has declared for the Nation."

"Has he indeed?" said the sergeant, and he sighed—as he always did. "It is a pity that the subaltern ranks should feel themselves so tied! Did any one try to kill the captain when he bolted?"

"Oh yes," said the messenger, "the usual thing; the guard wasted a few shots, but it was dark, and he got away."

"It's a long way to the frontier," said Boutroux, mixing in this cryptic conversation for the first time.

"You'll find it so, young man," said Sergeant Hamard dryly.

"That captain has gone before us into Galilee," said Boutroux.

The sergeant glanced at him slyly. "When you have been in the regiment a little longer," he said, "you will be a little more careful of your tongue."

To which the messenger added, "My wretched fellow, it is true, and remember it: treason and even desertion are most strictly forbidden in all below the rank of captain."

"And who is left in Angoulême," asked Hamard, "to look after us all?"

"The lieutenant, as I told you," said the other shortly; "but some one else has come: a Parliament man."

"A civilian?" said the sergeant, wondering.

"You may call him a civilian now," said the messenger in a musing tone, "but he has tremendous go, and it seems he commanded a regiment in his time. He drinks heavily at night; he sleeps well; and he is like a tornado in the morning."

"It's all Greek to me," said Hamard.

"You will understand well enough when we get to the town," answered the other, "and meanwhile I was to tell you this, only the charm of your conversation distracted me—when we get into Angoulême we obey orders, do you understand?"

"I've found it exceedingly difficult to do anything else during the last few months; show me my superior and I'll obey orders," answered the sergeant.

"Well, but that's the hitch; your superiors aren't there . . . and there may be some argument."

"That's what I feared."

"Now when you hear argument," continued the new-comer, "take my tip: I've been watching. If one tells you one thing, being a soldier, and the other tells you another, being a civilian to the eye, and a shouting and a swearing one, why, you will do well to obey the shouting and the swearing Parliament man. If you obey contrariwise, you're shot. Friend," he added, putting up a hand and laying it on the sergeant's bridle arm gently, " for God's sake tell everybody to be sensible."

" I have only three to tell," said the gentle-faced young sergeant.

"Then tell all the three and tell them in time," said the messenger brusquely, looking him full in the face. "For it will be a matter of shooting before noon ; and the people who shoot, wound, worse luck ! They have all the guns. It's the Parliament man that has the magazine."

When he had said this he proceeded to tell the whole tale. The news had come down five days before. The King was imprisoned ; there was God knew what government in Paris, but it was something fierce. The hussars had gone to pieces. The ranks were there, for the most part. The sergeants had held. There had been a few desertions, but the men were kept by pay and food and had not where to go. In all the squadrons not twenty privates had decamped, but the officers were gone, all but one—a lieutenant, a ranker. The rest had got off across country ; they were for the invader now the King had fallen. A man was there from the Parliament in Paris, and this man had full powers. The time had come, he repeated, for every one to do what he was told.

"Perrin," said the gentle Hamard to Boutroux, "do you ever pray?"

"Never!" said Boutroux decidedly.

"Do you ever toss a coin?"

"No, but when others do it I often cry heads or tails as the case may be."

"Why then, shall we pray or shall we toss a coin? for I fear that orders will be contradictory in Angoulême."

"If I were you," said Boutroux, "I would await the event, and after that I should pray, or at any rate I would offer up prayer or curses according to the result."

"There is not much comfort in that," said the sergeant, and for some time after both were silent.

The messenger from Angoulême trotted away again up the column on his wearied mount, and soon they saw before them the hill and the packed houses and the domes of the town.

The guard, as they came up to the gate of Angoulême, sent forward two men who quietly asked for a password and were given it. As the detachment came in they noted that the guard did not salute, and it seemed to them that there were very few men at the gate. The column was halted and bidden to dismount. All obeyed, including the officer who led them. And when this had been done, a short, swarthy man, nearly sixty years of age, with an animal determination in his face, his eyes bloodshot (from drink or from lack of sleep), but very fixed in their glance, came out suddenly from the guardroom at the gate.

There was an odd mixture of fear, respect, and annoyance in the way in which the soldiers received this figure.

He was dressed in knee-breeches, he wore no sword, he had a great riding-coat about him, of a dark green colour with brass buttons, on which were stamped the Fasces and the Axe. He had neither wig nor hat upon his head, but a mass of his own dark curling hair; and around his waist, making a mass of silken colour, was a tricolour scarf. It was tied in a huge bow above the sword hip—where was no sword—and the two tails of it hung down almost to his feet.

"In the name of the Nation," he said huskily, staring at the commander of the detachment, who stood before him without insolence or curiosity, awaiting what remained to be said. "I bring commands for whom I choose," he said brutally, "and I break what commissions I choose."

"There is no need for you to speak to me thus," said the commander of the detachment in an easy tone. "These with me are for the most part lads recruited during my mission to the south of this town ; the rest are of the old regiment. I only await orders."

The scarfed politician in the riding-coat, the tricoloured, was a little mollified, but he still spoke brutally.

"This captain who has bolted was one of yours ?"

"I don't even know which one it was," answered the lieutenant quietly.

The politician gave the name.

"Oh yes ! He was one of ours," said the lieutenant.

"And who else is going to bolt ?" asked the politician angrily.

"None that I know of, sir," said the officer gravely. "As for my men, they have come here bringing in the recruits to drill . . . and we take orders from Paris," he concluded.

"Ah," said the politician with a big breath, "you take orders from Paris ?" He looked the soldier up and down. "I know what soldiering is, mind you !"

"So I should have thought," said the cavalry

officer in answer. "In the line, I should say?" he added.

"No damned insolence!" shouted the other, suddenly firing up. "In the guns!"

"Well, then, in the guns."

"Well, then, in the guns," mimicked the politician, mocking him, "and in the guns we stood no nonsense. . . . Do you know that you have no colonel?"

"Since when?" said the chief of the detachment.

"The devil knows," answered the politician with an unpleasant laugh. "But the regiment and you others were to concentrate at Poitiers."

The cavalry-man nodded.

"Well," said the other with a sniff, "he had gone—bolted—by the time I came through."

The cavalry-man nodded again.

The politician grew exasperated. "I don't know whether you know more of it than you care to say, but do you know what strength there is in Poitiers?"

"There are not quite six hundred sabres to command, when all the detachments have come in, counting the recruits. I have the count correctly enough."

"You know what I mean," said the politician

surlily, but with a flash in his eye. "Who is to command your six hundred sabres?"

"If the colonel is gone," said the other calmly, "the senior officer."

"Well, my lad," answered the deputy coarsely, "that's you."

They looked at each other in mutual anger, with disgust and contempt upon the side of the soldier, and a little hidden fear of consequences upon the side of the civilian ; for that civilian was there alone unguarded, with nothing but the authority of the Parliament behind him. . . . "You understand me?" he asked. "I have the commissions in my pocket, and I can make and unmake. Will you take it on?"

"I do what I am told," said the soldier shortly. "Who are there here in Angoulême?"

"Three more detachments and perhaps a hundred recruits," said the other. "You must drill them on the way. You have heard what has happened in Paris?"

The cavalry-man answered that he had heard.

"How long will it take you to go to Poitiers?"

"Can I have remounts?" asked the officer.

"Can your recruits ride them?" retorted the politician.

"They will have to," said the officer patiently. "If you get me remounts I can be there upon the evening of the second day. But once there I must be able to fill my stables again and to pick and choose."

"Oh, you'll do that all right," said the other roughly. "We can gather horses by the hundred from the lunatics who have been rising under the priests thereabouts. Oh!" he went on, laughing hoarsely, "every man that comes out with his nag for the Pope is a beast for us, and sometimes a recruit as well. . . . We turn 'em in! There's some use in rebels!" At this point he jerked his thumb for the officer to follow him, and they went together into the guard-room. A little while after the soldier came out with the expression of a man who has eaten bitter fruit and has made up his mind.

He mounted and gave orders that all his command should mount. He dispatched two soldiers with orders, and in a few minutes there were gathered in the great place of the town quite three hundred mounted men; a hundred of them were still in their civilian clothes, sitting awkwardly in their knee-breeches or with trousers tied with string at the knee.

Boutroux filed in with the rest. There was

plenty of jostling and cursing and orders both whispered and shouted; but in the long run some sort of formation was got together. The two trumpeters sat their horses before the line in the square. The crowd of the town had begun to gather in the corners of the big open space to watch what might be toward; they laughed at the fellows in the civilian rags and they derided such a show. The officer who had commanded Boutroux's detachment and the recruits on the march from the south, and who had just held his conversation with the commissioner from the Parliament, rode up to where the trumpets were and faced the men. He had one lieutenant at his side; the sole remaining one was at the head of the formation. He gave the order.

"Now that the men are assembled," said he to a sergeant, "you can tell them to sound the assembly."

"Yes, my Captain," said the man.

"*Colonel!*" said the other, looking at him and very nearly forgetting discipline so far as to smile.

"Yes, my Colonel," stammered the man again with wide eyes. He rode up to the trumpets.

"The assembly and the regimental call," he said.

"Without the colonel?" asked the trumpet sergeant-major sullenly.

The sergeant moved his head imperceptibly towards the young officer still in his lieutenant's uniform, who sat his horse alone and looked down that long line. "That's the new colonel," he whispered.

"God help us all in the hussars!" answered the trumpet sergeant-major, and he gave the order.

The two men lifted their trumpets and sounded the assembly and the regimental call, giving that flourish at the end with their instruments which was due to a colonel's command.

As this ceremony—which was symbolic and decisive of the regiment's adhesion to the Revolution in Paris—took place, the Parliamentarian came up towards the new young colonel at the head of this command. He was swaggering and rolling on his feet, his tricoloured sash was still about him, and his way was marked by long rolls of popular cheers. Two cavalry-men on foot, with drawn swords, went with him. He came across the broad, open empty space, still swaggering, stopped near the officer, set his feet wide apart, and said,—

"Colonel, that is but half your command; the other half awaits you at Poitiers."

The officer gravely saluted.

"I will ask you, when the men are dismissed and quartered, to help me draw up a list of promotions. We must have a cadre. The commissions must be filled."

"It is simple enough," said the officer in a low voice. "I know the best of the non-commissioned officers here, and you can fill the list from no other source."

"We don't only want the best soldiers," growled the politician.

"I will talk to you of the rest," said the other guardedly.

"And what of making sergeants in the place of those we take for commissions?"

"I would have the new commissioned officers decide on the recommendations," said the colonel of half an hour's standing.

He sent another order; the trumpets rang out again, and confusedly jumbled at first, but at last disentangled, the whole line of veterans, of young soldiers, and of recruits—a few volunteers as well —broke up into their separate troops and sought the various streets of the city in which they were quartered.

The politician and the new-made colonel went off together to the chief hotel of the place, right on the big square; the one was still swaying on foot, with his great three-coloured scarf about him, the other soldierly upon his horse. There was an omen in that sight, and many who saw it knew that at last the army would rule the Republic. But for the moment the army took orders from Parliament as an army should ; and this new chief of the regiment went in to draw up his list of subordinates. Save for him and two bewildered lieutenants, there was not as yet a single man of commissioned rank to deal with all those hundreds.

CHAPTER XIII.

*In which the Girondin, though by no means yet
a Soldier, becomes very certainly a Sergeant;
and in which a Chivalrous Fellow strikes a
Blow for the Crown.*

BOUTROUX'S mount was quartered in a stable
belonging to a corn merchant. The corn
merchant had come into that stable to see the horse
groomed, and also to see that nothing should be
stolen. Boutroux groomed with precision and
care, and as he groomed a sullen, swarthy sort
of fellow, quite thirty years of age, in the uniform
of the regiment—and a dirty uniform at that—said
to him,—

"You're wanted—you're wanted at the White
Pheasant."

"Where's that?" said Boutroux pleasantly.

"It's an inn," said the other more sullenly than
ever, "and be damned to you!"

"Friend," said Boutroux, "you are senior in

the service to me, but it will give me great pleasure to touch you up with something pointed, and perhaps my host will lend me a crowbar or, at the worst, a kitchen knife."

"Go to hell!" said the other; "you'll have more power than you want before morning to prod poor devils like me."

He went up to the horse and stroked it gently.

"I knew this beast before ever you were in the regiment," he added, lachrymose; and then, "Go on to the White Pheasant, and don't remember my words." So saying, he took over the grooming.

Boutroux asked of the corn merchant where the White Pheasant might be. The dirty little inn was pointed out to him on the other side of the road. He went in, still dressed in his peasant clothes, hopelessly travel-stained after the long march. There he saw six sergeants who, when he came in, made a loud and confused noise, and shouted at him words the meaning of which he could not guess at all. One of them made as though to throw wine over him, another half drew his sword and was repressed by a friend, but the rest laughed, all save one—and that one (Boutroux was very pleased to see) was his gentle friend of the marching days.

"Well, Perrin," he said, "I have nominated you."

"My friend," said the other, smiling his sad smile, "I presume that you can read and write?"

"Certainly," said Boutroux.

"Well, Perrin, if you will believe me, in the whole troop there is not one who can write a clear hand, and only eight that can read; and in your sergeants' mess you will find that you will be the only one who can copy a dispatch or keep accounts. That's the reason."

"It's all very odd!" said Boutroux.

"Revolutions always are!" said the other, and went out.

That night, though the quarrel had begun between the disappointed members of the mess and their new comrade, there was no time for quarrelling. At the moment when their drinking and quarrelling should have begun they were ordered to the town hall, and found there, in a new medley of uniforms, freshly-commissioned officers who were their former comrades, and whom now they must salute—men of the people unused to any command save that of gentlemen; and in the presence of these new and strange officers refraining with difficulty from incongruous laughter and the still more incongruous oaths of the barrack room.

They found the new sergeants of every sort

drawn suddenly from the ranks, and files of the new recruits who, all night long, were being passed through for accoutrement, and dressed as best they could be.

In the morning, after a night during which not one-third of the force had slept, the whole body—the new commissioned ranks, the accoutrement staff, the recruits, and the guards—were drawn up again in the market-place of Angoulême, all dressed as they should be, and very deceptive to the eye: a civilian might have taken them all for soldiers. For the remounts had been put under the most experienced men, and the recruits sat those old, tame, sleepy beasts which were called in the regiment "the Circus."

These scratch troops filed out, therefore, in some order in that early morning. There were few of the civilians about; the Commissioner from the Parliament was sleeping out his excess of the night before.

The hussars took the great northern road, halted at Mansle, but pushed on all that day to the place called White Houses, seeing the haste there was to reach Poitiers; and during the mid-day halt, and at the great halt at night, steadily the recruits were drilled. That force was moulded as were all the pressed forces of the Revolution in their thousands, swept up from countrysides, and

drilling on the march; and so it was to be for
twenty years.

But Boutroux (invaluable for his reading and
writing) was at the accounts of the foraging and
with the books; and in Poitiers, where there was
to be a concentration and a waiting for two days, he
had his room in barracks, and had already begun
to learn the trade.

The cavalry barracks in Poitiers were roomy,
and the more roomy for the draining of men to the
frontier. Counting the detachment which had thus
come in from the south there were not eight
hundred sabres in the whole place, although the
buildings were designed for a full brigade.

All the regiment was there, and a maimed troop
of Royal Allemand as well; there were fifty
or sixty of these puzzled foreign mercenaries with
silly empty flaxen heads, a little terrified at the
storm that raged all around them, but knowing
too well how the People had come to hate such
hired fellows as they were. These poor lads kept
to barracks for safety amid the taunts, and worse, of
the French regiment. Their officers had gone over
to the enemy months ago; nearly all their body
had been dissolved by revolt, by emigration, or by
disease far off upon the frontier, and they, alone,
who had been dispatched upon a local mission,

remained isolated here, in the centre of the country at Poitiers, terribly afraid. They were glad even to do the heavy work which their French fellow-soldiers forced upon them, making them a sort of slaves. They dared not go into the town, for the town was in a ferment : lying upon the very edge of the Royalist districts, its municipality and its more active citizens exhibited an exaggerated zeal for the Revolution and for the New World.

Here, in Poitiers, the men who had just come up from the south heard, for the first time, the whole story in detail : how the Tyrant and the Austrian woman, his wife, and the little Wolf-cub, their son, were held prisoners in the Temple; how the traitors and the aristocrats had been arrested in Paris ; how the People were now supreme. They heard that the armies on the frontier were crowded with volunteers ; they heard the suspicions of treason and the general officers' names cursed upon every side — Lafayette's in particular, an arch traitor—and there was more than one private of long standing who suggested to his fellows that the time had come for getting rid of officers altogether, especially of those new fellows dragged out of the ranks, whom all the cavalry detested ; but, oddly enough, the privates found that with such an access of liberty discipline was stronger than ever, and one drunken fellow, who had said a word too much, having been tied up all day, for a show, at the barrack gates, the rest grumbled less loudly.

Meanwhile Boutroux, under the name of Perrin, in the Chief's room, worked at his books, and every hour that he could he followed drill. Boutroux was Sergeant Perrin, and Sergeant Perrin worked much harder than any of the sleepy-eyed horses of "the Circus," and twenty times as much as any of the new horses of the remounts. He was assiduous. But, steeped in his work as he was, the huge fantasy of the thing struck him more and more with each new day; and at night, when he had done drinking with the others, he would, in spite of his fatigue, lie awake sometimes, wondering at this makeshift for an army : educated men—and he had read, if anything, too much—could not believe in it.

A colonel who had been a captain not a week before ! Subalterns lifted up at a moment's notice from all manner of places, most of them still thick with the speech of the barrack room, and still heavy with the slouch of the ranks ! Ranks weakened by a third at least, and that third filled up anyhow, with pressed peasants, foolish jingo clerks, runaway boys, and tramps who asked for nothing but food ;—all these grotesquely enough dressed in the true uniform of soldiers, and a desperate haste and energy, hours and hours of riding-school and drilling, trying to make something of the hotch-potch! He couldn't believe in it.

The enthusiasm of the town helped his cynicism, for all this Revolution talk, which he had played with in Bordeaux, seemed to him, at close quarters with the populace, a hopeless thing.

There were black flags hung out to symbolise the national danger; long tricoloured streamers pendent from the roofs and windows to symbolise the national resolve. Now and again there would go through the streets half-maniacal processions of women and boys shouting against the invasion; and twice during the few hours he had been in the place the house of one or another who had been marked for vengeance had been wrecked as a sympathiser with the King and with the Austrian. It was a madness.

He was so much a soldier already, was Sergeant Perrin, that he could not bear to see the two guns stationed stupidly and permanently in the square of the town, with theatrical civilian gunners (volunteers dressed up for a show) standing by them, two hours at a time, and matches in their hands.

But especially the Clubs vexed him. Oh, he knew what it was, the spouting in the Clubs! He had been through it all at Bordeaux! And that ceaseless rhodomontade and those perpetual great words of Humanity, though he only heard them reported or sounding through the open windows of the summer meetings in the halls of inns or dancing-places, disgusted him. He went on with his work: they would be sent to the frontier at last, they would be there within a month; and when they got there, well, they would be broken up and torn to pieces as "troops" of such a kind must be whenever they were met by true soldiers.

One thing was real to him and a friend in this hurried march of exile and of concealment. He had a horse, a horse of his own——a white horse by name Pascal.

They had given it him on his promotion——and it was worth nothing, it was old. Where it came from, whether a peasant in Vendée had bred him, or whether he was pressed or bought, or old in the service, Boutroux did not know.

This horse he made a friend and grew familiar with. At everything else in that hurried way north he wondered.

He marvelled that the Royalists made less

show.   He had been brought up in a house philosophical upon the man's side, hard clerical upon the woman's, but all its friendships and connections respectable.   He had imagined—as wealthy men, and young wealthy men especially, will do—that such an atmosphere was the atmosphere of the whole world ; and here, now in Poitiers at least, it seemed to have vanished altogether.   Where were they, the men who, before the revolt, had been ready to die for the King and for religion, and for all that the French had been ?   On the second night after his arrival in Poitiers he got some idea of where they were.

There was a coffee-house on the summit of that hill town close to the wide open space called the Place d'Armes ; it stood between the cathedral and the town hall, and here, even in that time, a little rest and seclusion could be found.

Few frequented it ; old clients and regular customers, snuffy men for the most part.   Boutroux took refuge there, not without precaution. He did not like to leave his comrades for as much as an hour in the day, and his need for learning his trade took all his time.   But to sit in that coffee-house for a few moments at evening when he was at leisure was a benediction to him.   So sitting there upon that second evening, reading vaguely a news-sheet come from Paris—a news-sheet very bitterly opposed to the new state of things and putting its opposition very plainly—so sitting and drinking wine, he was aware of a figure that had taken a chair opposite him and was watching him closely.

Boutroux's sword was hanging upon a hook behind him, he had his shako on his head, he had even kept his gloves upon his hands : he was in regulation dress, and had nothing to fear even if the stranger was some authority in mufti ; but he soon learnt that he had other things to deal with than the regiment alone.

The stranger put his right hand closed upon the table, called for wine himself, and when he had done so, giving a rapid glance at Boutroux, he said,—

"You are reading the news from Paris, sir ?"

Boutroux looked up, and as he did so he saw the clenched hand of the stranger open very rapidly and disclose a locket with a portrait upon it. It was the portrait of a fat, rather silly, goggle-eyed man in a blue coat, and there was a fleur-de-lis stamped across it. The hand shut again quickly. The stranger looked up at a corner of the ceiling unconcernedly and murmured, "You understand ?"

"Perfectly," said Boutroux, who understood nothing; but he had learnt for now a fortnight not to be off his guard. He judged the stranger skilfully with imperceptible glances, darted momentarily at him while he pretended to continue his reading. The stranger was dressed in a long, dark cloak fastened at the neck with a pin. He wore trousers strapped under the heel and tight fitting, and under them one could see the shape of riding-boots. His face was thin, long, and hatchet-like, his eyes deep-set, arched, and sad. Upon his head he wore a rather shabby old felt hat set at a challenging angle. He might have been a man off the stage or from the fair, but Boutroux judged him right: mad or sane, he was a rebel.

He opened his hand again with the same abrupt gesture and left it open a little longer this time, so that Boutroux could see the miniature which it held. As he did so, his face had about it a religious look: it was not quite sane.

In an awkwardness of this kind one must make up one's mind quickly, and Boutroux did so.

"You have a portrait of the King," he said simply.

"Yes," said the stranger with reverence and in a lower voice. "You are worthy of us; you call him by his name. Sergeant, by what you are reading you should be trusted."

"I have always been trusted," said Boutroux pleasantly, laying down the paper and looking full at his companion. "I have never been suspected, thank God, by any one in my life. I have done my plain duty as a soldier since, in my childhood, I was adopted by this regiment, in which my father served. But I am always willing to hear."

The stranger looked troubled. "I would not compromise any man," he said slowly, "but there are some of us who are determined to inflict a just punishment upon one who has committed treason."

Boutroux looked very grave. "Not of ours?" he said.

"Yes, of yours," said the stranger firmly. "The news has been sent us from Bordeaux by the Central Association. They have traced him, I am very, very sorry to say, to your corps."

"Who is 'him'?" said Boutroux with wide eyes. "What have I to do with this?"

"Nothing," said the stranger shortly, "except to do your duty as you boast to do. Your King is a prisoner, but he may yet be avenged. . . . In Bordeaux," continued the stranger, crossing his

legs and looking more indifferently than ever at
the corner of the ceiling, "a man upon whom
many of ours depended—at any rate, the friend of
many of ours—betrayed the cause. He joined the
Jacobins secretly, he raised them against his
own household (it is a damnable thing to have to
say, but he did so) ; his uncle and guardian, who
had befriended him, was arrested and now lies in
prison. He had already fled, by the 10th of
August, wisely, but the rabble had been warned by
him. . . . It is due to his treason that the Rebels
had time to hold the quays in Bordeaux, and that,
when the news of the rebellion came from Paris,
they had the shipping in their hands. That man,"
he ended simply and decisively, "must suffer
death."

"A man of such power," murmured Boutroux,
"could hardly remain hidden. He must be a
very master of men ! Was he young or old ?"

"Quite young," said the stranger pathetically,
"a mere boy—barely of age."

"Tut, tut," said Boutroux, "what powers do
not revolutions reveal ! "

"At any rate," said the stranger, cutting him
short, "he is in your regiment."

"I'm sorry to hear that," said Boutroux ; "he
will get promotion ; men of that sort always do."

"We may stop it first," said the other firmly. "I've said it before and I say it again, if we cannot save the Altar or the Crown, we can avenge them."

"By all means!" said Boutroux genially, calling for some more wine and offering it to the stranger. "What was his name?"

The man in the cloak pulled out a notebook and read as follows,—

"'Name, Boutroux, Georges. Probably adopted an alias. Of an offensive carriage; high, affected voice. Talkative. Can ride; if enlisted, probably in a cavalry regiment. Further traced beyond Chiersac, then lost. Reported by Melchior in cavalry barracks at Poitiers.' That was yesterday," said the stranger dolefully. "Poor Melchior was taken off to Paris yesterday upon some charge by these wolves."

Boutroux nodded and thanked God within his heart.

"I wish he were here, for he knew the traitor's face."

Boutroux rapidly sought in his mind for the name of any Royalist companion of his from Bordeaux who might conceivably know Poitiers. He suddenly remembered one.

"This Melchior," he said, looking steadily at

the other, "was Sarrant by his family name, I think?"

The stranger looked back as steadily.

"I shall not tell you," he said.

"You need not," said Boutroux lightly, "but he came round to quarters and he spotted your man. He told me his own name in case I ought to communicate with him."

"He *did!*" said the stranger delightedly. "Poor Melchior! You saw him? You grasped him by the hand?"

"Yes, sir," said Boutroux, with a choke in his voice. "I held him by both hands; he was an honest man!"

"Now I know that you will serve us!" said the tall, hatchet-faced one radiantly. "Can you take me to your barracks now? At once?"

Boutroux pondered within his mind. "You had better wait," he said, "until to-morrow morning at ten, about an hour before we relieve the guard. If you will come then, I will leave orders that the man shall be brought out to meet you as to meet a relative. You can take him away, and after that it is in your hands." He leaned over and whispered in the stranger's ear, "Many of us are with you." Then he wrote upon a piece of paper, "The person with the order from the colonel asks to see his nephew." "That is all you will have to say," he said, "but say it exactly so."

The stranger nodded mysteriously, and they parted friends.

Boutroux, as he went back to barracks, considered. "You are a more important man, Georges," he thought, "than I had imagined. It seems that you have become a legend in Bordeaux. The Royalists are after you in earnest; and if the Royalists, then, probably, also the Jacobins. . . . It was your fault, Boutroux, for being born the nephew of so wealthy a man. . . . And now I hear that he is in prison. I am sorry for that, though I should be glad if my aunt were there too! You are an important man, Boutroux," he mused as he went across the great open Place d'Armes, with his sword-hilt caught in his arm to prevent the scabbard from trailing, and as he went he gazed at the ground.

"You have fame, Boutroux," he continued to himself, "and you can see for yourself whether you like it or no. The Royalists are after you, and certainly the Jacobins. And as for the authorities, for the police, for the official fellows, if they still survive after the explosion of the last few days, why, they must in common decency be after you, for you killed a man. . . . Then there

is *her* family," he remembered as he got near the
gates of the barracks ; " there is the lady of the
coffee-stall, there is her mother, there is the cleric
in the cellar, and there is she who is dancing or
was dancing in Libourne. But," said he, looking
up to the stars as he neared the gate, " there is no
longer Miltiades : at least, not within hail."

And having so considered the situation, he
saluted the guard at the gate and went in, to lie
upon his bed as he was, booted and spurred.

CHAPTER XIV.

Showing the Advantage there is for a German, in the Profession of Arms, that he should know the French Tongue.

NEXT morning at dawn, when the roll had been called and the horses fed, Boutroux sent from his room for the corporal of the guard.

"A gentleman will come an hour before the guard is relieved," he said, "and will say that he has an order from the colonel to see a man in the regiment."

"Yes, Sergeant," said the corporal.

"The man he wishes to see," said Boutroux quietly, "is Meister of the Royal Allemand."

"He is in the cells, Sergeant," said the corporal stiffly.

"Then," said Boutroux without turning a hair, "the man he wants to see is not Meister, but Fritz."

"Yes, Sergeant," said the corporal with an impassive face. He went back across the courtyard to the guard-house, but Boutroux threw open the window and called after him,—

"And if Fritz is dead, some other of the Germans. And if that other is in hospital, then any other one. Only give him a German."

"Yes, Sergeant," said the corporal, saluting, for it is the custom in that service for each rank to salute the rank above it, and not officers only.

Next morning, just before ten o'clock struck, Boutroux, his arms crossed upon a window sill, watched with huge delight the advent of the cloaked stranger. His tall figure came across the Place d'Armes, stalking grandly; his thin fanatic face was determined and full of mission. He came up to the guard.

"The gentleman who has leave from the colonel to see one of the soldiers," he said stiffly.

Boutroux was out at once, and with the corporal of the guard he fetched the German. The German was frightened; he knew little French; he thought that yet another practical joke was to be played upon him, and he was right. But Boutroux sustained him with kindness.

"That gentleman," he said, pointing to the cloaked figure outside, "will have a word with

you. Whatever happens maintain the honour
of your regiment, for there is not much of it
left—I mean of your regiment." And he handed
over Fritz, whom the stranger looked up and
down with a terrible eye. Boutroux sauntered
out toward them.

"Here is your friend, sir," he said, "but his
work begins again in half an hour, and we should
like him back."

"Leave him to me," said the stranger with
an exaggerated courtesy, "leave him to me,
Sergeant"—and they walked off together; the
German infinitely pleased to be out of quarters,
and to be going on an errand with so fine a
gentleman.

As the two went together across the market
square, Boutroux summoned a little Parisian
fellow, short and extraordinarily swagger, and,
calling him by the vilest name he could think
of for the moment, asked him whether he would
like an hour in town.

The man's eyes brightened. "I am in the
stables from now till five, Sergeant."

"I'll let you off," said Boutroux.

The man, still standing stiff, answered with a
little hesitation : "But, Sergeant, it was Sergeant
Maurat who told me."

"Never mind Sergeant Maurat," said Boutroux; "I'll make it all right with him. There's a regimental service on," he said mysteriously, "and I've picked you out because of your intelligence."

The Parisian was pleased.

"And I may also tell you," he added, "that intelligent or not you will be no use in another sixty seconds, and if you are later than that you will very probably be lost in the enterprise on which you are to be sent."

The Parisian wondered, but only answered: "I'm not dressed to pass the guard."

"I'll do that," said Boutroux quietly. He walked with the man past the guard into the open square, nodding at the sergeant of the guard as much as to say, "This is a message," and they were not challenged.

The German and his tall romantic captor had by this time nearly reached the further end of the Place d'Armes, and were at the mouth of a narrow street which leads out of it towards the steep northern escarpment of the town.

"You see those two?" asked Boutroux.

"Yes, Sergeant," said the Parisian.

"Well, all you have to do is to find out where they go. Once you have seen them into a house, don't leave it; and if the Royal Allemand doesn't

come out in half an hour, run back and report
to me."

The Parisian was going to ask whether there
were written orders ; but being a Parisian he
thought better of it, and he went off smartly
across the square, catching his sword under his
arm and putting some pace into his walking.
He was soon but a few yards behind his chase :
he could slacken his pace and watch their movements more discreetly.

Meanwhile the tall Royalist, who had sworn
to avenge his cause, and the German, with the
happy smile of release and of an hour's liberty
upon his face, had begun to misunderstand each
other.

While they were still crossing the Place d'Armes
the elder man, the civilian, said nothing, and
the young German had done no more than to
express in broken French, and in three or four
words continually repeated, how glad he was
to be picked out for town service, and how ready
he was to accomplish it, whatever it might be.
His honest, dull eyes and fat, fair face were full
of pleasure. The other answered nothing except
once in a murmur to the effect that disguises
were useless. And the German, a little worried
by such a rebuke, stumped on to the opening

of the narrow street. Once they were within it his guide said to him,—

"I warn you of one thing; it will be best to reply simply and truthfully, for whatever our determination may be, truth will save you and untruth will undo you."

His companion, who understood no more of this than of so much Greek, smiled largely and said "Zo," adding the title "Captain," which conveyed to him an expression of the highest compliment. The Royalist quickly looked at him again.

"You are beginning badly!" he said sharply.

The German nodded cheerfully. "Zo!" said he again.

"Well," said his companion, setting his mouth, "you may mock me now and I must bear with it; but it will not last long!"

They turned off the narrow street into a still narrower court, at the end of which was a green wooden door with elaborate old hinges of beaten iron, and above the coping of the high wall on either side of which appeared garden trees. Some fifteen yards within the garden a small house stood. The faded green shutters were closed against the August sun, and there was no sound of movement within.

The Parisian, when the two of them had turned down this courtyard, peeped carefully round the corner of it and saw them enter; he saw the elder man open the garden door with a key and motion his companion in. The door shut behind them and there was no further sound.

The Parisian bethought him that a man standing still in uniform and watching one particular door from down the length of a courtyard would, in such a town and at such a moment, be very much at a loss to explain himself if any one of half a dozen interests had cause to suspect him. He might be asked a question by a spy of the police, by a chance member of the Jacobin Club, by a plain citizen out for adventure and suspicious of all men—as plain citizens at that moment were. Being a Parisian, the Parisian thought quickly, and his decision was soon taken. He compared the risk of a row with his captain in barracks—or even with his sergeant—and the risk of a row with civilians now that all the world was at war, and he very rightly decided in favour of a row (if need be) with civilians. One was hardly safe anywhere except in the Army. He had burned his boats, or rather Sergeant Boutroux had burned them for him, by going out of quarters without due leave.

He pulled down the jugular strap of his shako, which is the sign of service ; he fastened it tightly under his chin ; he pulled his face into an expression of official determination and solemnity ; he drew his sword, sloped it at the regulation angle, and began very solemnly to pace the courtyard to and fro, up to the garden gate ten yards, and back again ten yards, with the method and regularity of a sentry.

"God knows," he thought, "what I am watching, but this kind of thing guarantees a man."

So regular a performance produced its effect. His methodical and ringing steps had not accomplished their third turn when a window opened from one of the three houses above the narrow courtyard, and a fat man in his shirt-sleeves, a butcher, looked out and hailed him.

"Who's under arrest?" he asked.

The cavalry-man did not answer. He continued to pace solemnly as before.

"I don't mean to ask any awkward questions," added the butcher sullenly, and then for a space was silent, watching the pacing figure quite three minutes without a word. At last he continued, "Look here, Citizen, it's no good playing the mummy ; we know who lives in that house better than you do, and if the colonel in command has put them under arrest, the People will be with you. They're suspect. You understand ?" He winked beefily.

The Parisian, if he understood, gave no sign of it. He did not so much as look at his interlocutor, but continued to pace up and down. And every time he arrived at the green garden door, with its beaten iron hinges, he halted theatrically, turned right about face, settled his hand again within the hilt of his sabre, readjusted its angle, and took on again his stiff but military performance.

" Oh, we know you ! " said the butcher as he came up again, "but you needn't make a mystery of it. I tell you the People are with you ; and they're with your colonel. But if you do make a mystery of it," he added a little threateningly, "the People may have reason to ask questions."

The self-appointed sentry turned away without a movement of recognition and began pacing again towards the door.

Another window opened, and this time a woman's head appeared : she was shrill, but her shrillness was addressed not to the sentry but to the butcher.

" Put your head in, fat Thomas ! " she screamed. " If there are scandals in our street, it will be the worse for you ! You are drunk ! "

" I am not drunk ! " said the butcher.

"You *are* drunk!" repeated the woman, her voice rising; "you always are by noon! Put your head in!"

"Put your head in yourself, old Sacristy Candle Eater," said the butcher, conveying in that epithet a contempt at once for women and for religion. "Put your head in and mumble prayers, or better still go and draw more wine for the priest you are hiding."

"He lies!" shrieked the woman to the sentry; "do not believe him."

The Parisian paced on as methodically as ever.

"There is no priest in this house! And as for wine, he knows more of it than we do! He is a butcher," she added by way of explanation, "and a drunkard."

"A drunkard!" shouted the butcher, his attention now withdrawn from the first object of his curiosity, "a drunkard, did you say? Wait a moment!" His head disappeared.

The woman, without waiting for the onslaught that might possibly follow, had begun to shout for aid, other windows opened over that courtyard, there was all the prospect of the noise and the inquiry which the cavalry-man had particularly wished to avoid—and which he met by continuing his stolid pacing—when from within the little house behind the garden other and more significant noises arose : mixed with loud protests in broken French, and in a German accent, protests intermingled with plain German oaths, came sharp commands to be silent. The occupants of the houses had come down into the courtyard. There were a dozen of them ; the butcher in the excitement forgot his quarrel with the old lady next door ; a man who protested above the din that he was a printer and needed sleep ; a companion who told him that night was the time for sleep and day the time for revolution, and with them the whole company had begun an intolerable hubbub—when the Parisian, seeing that things were looking ugly, turned popular attention in what was, for him, the right direction.

"Citizens," he said, speaking for the first time, "I'm on duty before this door. I shall go through it, and the safety of the Army is in the hands of the People."

They applauded without any more notion of what he meant than had he himself. He went to the door, tried it, found it shut, and banged at it with the hilt of his sabre. From within, the loud protests of the German, who seemed from the sound of his voice to be near some door or window of the house, and half outside it, and who was scuffling desperately, reached them. Then did the Parisian rise to the height of his genius.

"Open!" he bawled.

"Who's there?" asked a low voice within, while at the same time the keyhole was occupied by a human eye.

"The Army!" said the Parisian, as though he had behind him all the battalions of the defence.

By way of answer the eye retreated from the keyhole, two bolts were shut, and something heavy was heard being dragged up against the door.

Meanwhile the protests of the German had sunk into a muffled bawling, the noise of a violent struggle drew further and further within the house, and the cavalry-man, forgetting all prudence, or rather deciding instinctively which was the safer side, took a plunge. He turned round upon the excited gathering, which was swollen now by new-comers running up from every side and pouring into the courtyard, and he shouted,—

"Citizens, Austrian conspirators are at work within, and I must summon you against them!"

With these words half a dozen of the younger men began to help him in his efforts against the door: it would not yield, but with the rapid instinct which was the note of that time three formed a platform, lowering their heads against their crossed and linked arms against the wall ; two others climbed upon their shoulders ; the cavalry-man, sheathing his sword (he being much the lightest of them), climbed up upon these again, and bidding others follow, he dropped into the garden beyond.

Those outside heard the noise of an assault, the cries of the soldier as he struck with his sword against not metal but wood, and one young man after another, scrambling over the human ladder, dropped into the garden after him to his aid.

What they saw was what they had expected : the Parisian was standing with his back to one of the garden trees, a table was kicked over before him, and a chair broken ; he was swinging his sword in circles to preserve an open space ; half a dozen civilians were attempting to close with him, all known to the crowd for Royalists ; a man in another uniform (with which the populace were unfamiliar) was held close by two captors and was struggling hard ; at the bolts of the door stood a man-servant more than a little flurried.

One of the last to drop over the wall grasped with a rapidity which any general officer might have envied the key of the position : he hit the servant in the stomach, hard, and while that domestic was recovering, he unbolted the door and let in the flood.

The populace poured in roaring; every man fought with his neighbour, but on the whole the direction of the fighting was against the inmates of the house, and after ten seconds of rough and tumble the two soldiers were standing apart, the Royalist occupants of the garden were upon the ground, handkerchiefs and shreds of clothing were binding their hands—and the position was taken.

Once more the Parisian rose to the height of his mission; he told the German rapidly in barrack slang to fall in, and as there was nothing to fall in to, the German stood behind him, hoping for deliverance. He begged the noble and enthusiastic populace to bring their prisoners behind him, and at the head of a procession which dragged those unwilling Royalists captive, not without blows, across the Place d'Armes, he led them to quarters.

Arrived at the gate he was ready to deliver another speech, for his success had slightly inflamed him, when the guard turned out and with a fine impartiality arrested the whole populace, Royalists, and German. The fifty or so who had accompanied the prisoners, the prisoners themselves, the

German in a vast confusion, and all save the cavalry-man, to whom the movement was due, were hurried pell-mell into the guard-room, lined on the benches, and a guard set over them, while the sergeant went for orders, beckoning the cavalry-man to follow him.

The Parisian set his sabre stiffly again and marched by the side of the sergeant with all the strength of martial authority displayed.

"You will have to answer for this," said the sergeant shortly.

"I'm ready," said the Parisian.

In the orderly room they found the young and recently promoted lieutenant, Hamard, Boutroux's companion in the early march.

"We have prisoners, Lieutenant," said the sergeant.

The young lieutenant rose and proceeded with them to the guard-room. He found there a number of townsmen protesting against their arrest; two old gentlemen very nicely dressed but tumbled all to pieces, one with blood upon his hatchet face, and both bound; their servant also bound; and looking more foolish than ever, the German.

"What is all this?" asked the lieutenant, smiling.

"I do not know, sir," said the sergeant of the guard.

"You don't know?" said the lieutenant.

"No, sir; they came tumbling in with this man" (he pointed to the Parisian, who kept his jugular under his chin and still had his sword strictly to his shoulder); "he can tell you."

And the Parisian told.

"My Lieutenant," he said, "Sergeant Perrin will explain. As for me I only watched, and I guarded a door that I was told to guard. As I guarded it I heard proposals against the State which shall be answered later. I know neither the rights nor the wrongs of it, but I thought it my duty to bring them all here."

"You thought it your duty," said the lieutenant, musing, and with all the appearance of understanding the thing from top to bottom, "to bring them all here. You did well."

"They are of the faction," said the butcher; "they were conspiring against the People."

"They were suborning the Army," said a lad not yet of age for arms. "It was I who captured him," and he jerked his thumb at one of the old Royalist gentlemen, who told him that he was a liar.

The lieutenant turned to the German, and the

German attempted an explanation, but his French failed him.

The lieutenant sent the sergeant of the guard for the chief of the detachment of Royal Allemand, and the chief of the detachment of the Royal Allemand came. He was an enormous man from Alsace, German in figure, French in bearing, already sober, but recently arisen from sleep. He had a voice that rolled like thunder, and his examination consisted in a harangue.

"So you've been meddling with one of my men," he said as he strode in. He shouted it indifferently at the assembled civilians.

"We've rescued him," said the butcher.

"Hold your tongue!" shouted the German, his French glib and perfect, but his German accent very strong. "You've been meddling with one of my men because he's a foreigner! It's happened before, and it will be the worse for you! We won't stand it! We won't have it! We did for ten of you who acted thus a week ago!"

The German humbly put in a word in his native tongue to the effect that the honest fellows had rescued him from sudden death.

"You shall suffer with the rest," roared the officer; "you were out of quarters without leave!"

Hamard slipped off and came back again in a few moments.

" Sergeant Perrin has gone to explain matters to the colonel," he said ; "we must wait till he returns with authority." The prisoners swung their heels, the guards guarded, the two officers stalked up and down outside.

To these a private came running : "A corporal and four men to the colonel, and the prisoners with them."

Ten minutes later the corporal and the four men were leading their prisoners across the square to the town hall, there to guard them till the magistrate should come. The populace had no doubt that the Royalists whose house they had stormed would be referred to Paris, for such was the mood of that time.

Quarters were quiet again. The lieutenant went up towards stables ; he saw Sergeant Perrin standing vaguely and biting a straw. As he came up, the sergeant came to attention and saluted.

" What did the colonel say, Sergeant ? "

" My Lieutenant, he said the Royalists were fools ! "

" Right !   And what did he say of the mob ? "

" My Lieutenant, he said the mob were fools ! "

"Right! And what did he say of Fritz and your hussar—for you were seen to send that hussar?"

"My Lieutenant, he said they were both great fools."

"Right! And what did he say of you?"

"He suspended his judgment, sir. Those were his very words."

"I am glad of it," said Lieutenant Hamard thoughtfully; "he might have suspended you. Dismiss!"

CHAPTER XV.

In which an Ostler is too Political.

NEXT day by the relief of the guard it was known that the conspirators, the Austrians were off to Paris, to the High Court under guard; the mob that had captured them congratulated and recompensed; and the Army formally thanked for its zeal. A little after noon the news went round quarters that on the morrow they would march for the east, and it was good news for all of them. The force was beginning to get some shape into it, hugger-mugger though it was, and Poitiers was getting too political if there was one thing the army hated it was politics. To be seized round the neck by market-women and told that you were adored for opinions you never held; or, when what you most needed was sleep after a long day and drinking, to be cheered before a company

of singers and told that you were the bulwark
of the country ; or worse still, to receive a
violent blow in a dark passage and to have
yourself called a traitor by some one whose views
upon the State you did not know and who
might very well be in agreement with you—
these were the things the young soldiers could
not bear.

The prospect of active service drew them
together and lifted their hearts, and they were
glad to be off again to the east, whither they
were bound by their trade of fighting ; and
Boutroux—to whom every march away from the
south was so much added safety—welcomed it
most ; but he had another hedge before him.

That same afternoon, as he was looking to
the grooming of the horses in the barrack square,
a civilian, an ostler, had sauntered by. He was
a man with a strong, very unpleasant face, one
who seemed moreover to take strange liberties
with quarters and yet whom no one seemed
to dare reprove ; he had come in on some
pretext and passed Sergeant Boutroux a certain
word in an undertone ; it was a word Boutroux
had known exceedingly well — once, weeks or
days ago, in Bordeaux — too well. It struck
him like a sentence of law when he heard it.

It was the password of the Club on the night when that little affair in Bordeaux had occupied his former wealthy leisure.

Boutroux, as he heard that word, had no time for plan or forethought. He replied with the counter password : he murmured to the ostler, as that impudent fellow lounged away, " *The Human Race*," a simple enough phrase and big enough in all conscience, but it did its work ; the ostler lounged back again. The nearer he got, and the better Boutroux could look at him, the less he liked his face.

The men were grooming the horses in a long line ; Boutroux stood there overlooking them, now calling out to one or another whom he thought was slacking in his work, or to a recruit who did not seem yet to have learned it. The civilian ostler had little business there ; but Boutroux, having heard the password and having given the countersign, would not ask questions. The ostler said in a low tone,—

" Sergeant Perrin, we know who you are."

" That is not difficult," said Boutroux, keeping his temper and his colour too.

" Shall I tell you the story in case you do not want to help us ? " continued the ostler in that same undertone, so that no one else could hear, and gazing, as the sergeant did, at the men's work and the line of horses.

"I am quite indifferent," said Boutroux, pulling from his trousers pocket a little leaden medal on which was stamped the triangle and the two pillars of the Society. The ostler as rapidly showed in his hand, open for a moment, a similar symbol, pocketed it again, and continued,—

"These trinkets are not only useful to protect a man : sometimes they damn him ! "

"If he betrays the Brethren," said Boutroux, using the old ritual reply.

The ostler was silent, but in a moment or two he said : "When do the men water the beasts ?."

"They've pretty well done their grooming now," said Boutroux. "I shall be giving the order soon. Why ? "

"Because I can say what I have to say better when the clatter of hoofs begins."

"Oh, I understand . . ." said Boutroux, and in a moment he had given the order. The men put down their curry-combs and their brushes, one and another gave a lingering pat to his animal ; then at the second order every man had scrambled or vaulted on to his mount, and was taking it off in file to the drinking-troughs.

The clatter of the horse-shoes upon the paving of the barrack-yard was loud, and the ostler could say what he had to say at his ease ; he said it shortly.

"Sergeant Perrin," said the ostler, watching the receding line of horses with a critical eye, and walking side by side with Boutroux as he strolled behind the cavalcade to see that the watering was in order, "Sergeant Perrin, I have told you that we know who you are."

"I . . ." began Boutroux.

The ostler gave an impatient shake of the head. "When I have done you will see whether there is any need for you to talk," he said brutally. "Your mother lives in the long farm-house upon the highroad on the Bordeaux side of Chiersac. She is an old witch of the King's and she hobnobs with the priests."

"She is not my mother," said Boutroux shortly.

"Well then, your step-mother," said the ostler impatiently.

"That's more like it, damn her !" answered Boutroux quietly.

"Just after the Tyrant was taken and the Tuileries stormed by the People, a man who had been hiding in the wood came to your house, and your mother harboured him."

"That's right," said Boutroux, beginning to see daylight.

"You, Sergeant Perrin, were down for enlistment, but you wanted some one to drive the horse back, and that some one was the man your step-mother harboured."

"It's perfectly true," said Boutroux stolidly.

"He drove back with the cart, and you took the oath that evening."

"I did," said Boutroux.

"The Brethren in Bordeaux," continued the ostler in a lower and rather graver voice, "have sent us the report, and what you are required upon your oath to answer is this : Where that man is and how he may be taken."

Boutroux thought a moment. The rustic Perrin who had driven him was a member of the Society. So much was clear. He was affiliated in spite of his mother, and the Society believed him to be that rustic. So much else was clear. That the Society wanted Boutroux, to kill him, Boutroux knew. The last of the horses was watered in its turn ; the file was clattering back towards the stables. He swung slowly after them, the ostler by his side looking at him fixedly with his eyes and eagerly with his mind.

"I don't mind what happens to the man,"

said Boutroux at last, a bitter note in his voice. "I'll give every help."

"You're bound to," said the ostler gravely; "but you'll be the more willing when I tell you what he did."

"What did he do?" asked Boutroux.

"He betrayed the Club in Bordeaux, and he killed a man on faction—one of his Brothers in the Society."

"Did he, by God!" said Boutroux.

"He did, by God!" answered the ostler. "There were plenty of things that night which no man could understand. The man's name was Boutroux. He went to a meeting of the Society; he was with the Brethren and the Section—it's all one there—and he tried to buy off his old uncle."

"Did they take his money?" said Boutrou. gently.

The ostler spat. "I don't know, and I don't care," he said, "but anyhow the Executive ordered the uncle's house to be guarded; he'd had a meeting of the traitors there that night. When Boutroux found that that was known, he killed the man on guard. At first we thought he was hiding in his uncle's house, but he wasn't. We've made sure of that, Sergeant."

"How ?" said Boutroux.

"Oh well," said the ostler, laughing, "the report says that the old chap's in jail; the People went through the house, you may lay to it. It's as empty as a barn to-day."

Boutroux was on the point of saying, "And where's the old lady ?" but he caught the words on his lips, and turned them. "And where's what you want me to do ?" he said, and as he said it he thought of that familiar house, stripped, ransacked, looted, old Nicholas dead perhaps, or more probably flying; fire perhaps upon the walls of his own room, and the great stone halls deserted altogether; the tall panes of the windows broken, the ironwork of the gilt lantern twisted, and the carved oaken doors broken in. He tasted the taste of his exile, and he did not love that old hag of the roadside or her son any better as he thought of it.

"I told you," said the ostler shortly, "that you've got to tell us where the fellow is; for you know . . ." he added, his voice becoming threatening.

The horses were in the stables; the men had gone back to their barrack rooms, their work accomplished; the stable guard were going their

9 a

rounds, tossing the hay into the mangers
Boutroux laid a hand upon the ostler's shoulde
more firmly than that civilian liked.

"Brother What's-your-name," he said, "I an
not answerable to you : I am answerable to th
Society. Do they meet to-night ? If so, tell m
where, or take me there."

"Have you got night leave ?" said the ostler
"for you will need it."

"I will try to get it," Boutroux replied. "
shall probably have to be back by midnight."

He made an appointment with the Jacobi
to meet him at the gate that evening, and wit
that appointment in mind he went off to as
for leave.

It fell to the duty of Lieutenant Hamard t
grant leave for the troop.

"Friend Perrin," he said gently as Boutrou
came in, "I would have you stand at attention
it is more respectful."

And Boutroux, who was already standing a
attention, stiffened himself. The lieutenant looke
him up and down.

"Your shako is on one side," he said.

The sergeant straightened it.

"And now," said the lieutenant, "it is o
the other."

The sergeant put it back again.

"Who cleaned the hilt of your sword?"

"I did, my Lieutenant," said Sergeant Perrin.

"When I was a sergeant," murmured the lieutenant, "I always made a soldier do that. Times are changing. What do you want?"

"Night leave, sir."

"You can't have it: they will call the roll before dawn."

"Midnight leave, sir."

"If the captain will give you midnight leave, I will have it sent to you. Dismiss!" he concluded gently. It was his favourite word.

Boutroux swivelled round and left the room. He knew he should find the leave on his table within an hour, and he did. The ostler, the Brother, came up to the gate of quarters at the fall of evening, and they went off through the town together.

CHAPTER XVI.

*In which the Brethren of Equality and Frater-
nity are led to behave in a Manner mos
Unfraternal and Inequitable; and in whic
the Children of Light are unmercifull
Bamboozled.*

THE Brethren within Poitiers (their lodg
had a name I forget) had met in the hal
once dedicated for a thousand years to St. Hilary
that ancient bishop of the town, but for th
moment called after virtue pure and simple: i
was the Hall of Virtue.

It was packed with some three hundred o
the Brethren of every rank and kind, but fo
the most part men of the middle class of th
town — one or two women among them — and
on the raised platform at one end the bureau
the President and the secretaries, under whom
these public gatherings were organised. The

ostler asked Boutroux what he should tell the President.

"Tell him," said Boutroux, "that when he comes to my business, if he will call upon me I will speak of the Bordeaux business. My speech will do all that is wanted of me."

The ostler looked at him a little doubtfully, and went off to convey that message to the officials upon the platform. Boutroux took a chair, sitting there in his uniform, his hands upon the hilt of his sword and his scabbard between his knees. His mouth was firm; he felt moved to take his revenge.

The President was a little nervous man, bald and spectacled, a doctor; he opened the proceedings with such a speech as Boutroux was now familiar with, a speech like any one of dozens of others which he had heard in the Society at Bordeaux. But there was something more fierce about it and more secure, for in the interval Liberty had conquered.

The plaster busts which, in imitation of the mother-society in Paris, the Jacobins of Poitiers had set round their hall wore, every one of them, the red Phrygian cap which the worthy spinners of the North of England turned out by the thousand, indifferently, for brewers' draymen in their own country, for Republicans in Gaul, and indeed for any one who cared to buy that type of headgear.

There was the bust of Mirabeau, the bust of Priestley, the bust of Rousseau, the bust of Brutus, and the busts of other of the Jacobin saints, each wearing in a gallant fashion the red cap cocked over its left ear, and listening to the rhetoric of Freedom.

Boutroux himself heard in the ten minutes of that speech more of what had happened in Paris than all the gossip of the march and the villagers and the mobs in the towns told him. He heard how the palace had been stormed, he understood what Government now held the country. He heard the great name of Danton cheered as a minister and a man in power, and he heard—as violent as ever, but with a note of authority which hitherto such harangues had not possessed—the denunciation of treason.

Another speech followed, and another; there were questions from the Brethren, answered to the best of the officials' knowledge, wild suspicions expressed and calmed, wilder proposals listened to and ignored.

At last his turn came.

The President told the assembly that the plot

in Bordeaux for the murder of the patriots upon the very eve of the People's victory in Paris had been discovered, and that among them that night was a true Friend of the People, a man of that region, who would unmask the principal traitor, who would speak to them upon the nature of his treason, and who would later give the Executive all the evidence that was needed for finding the miscreant and giving him his just deserts. As he concluded he looked at the young soldier and called him to the platform.

"Sergeant Perrin!" he said, introducing him nervously. "Sergeant Perrin . . . of the hussars now passing through this town and on their way to chastise the kings who have dared to invade the territory of freemen."

There was loud, foolish, and violent applause. The sight of the uniform as the young man stepped up above them, with the swagger he had so soon learned, and his sword caught under his left arm, frenzied the Brethren; the rare sisters of the Brethren were more frenzied still.

As Boutroux waited for that storm of cheering to lessen he wondered whether he had the capacity to speak as he desired to speak. He soon found, as he measured his first words, that the task was not beyond him. The night helped him, and the enthusiasm, and the numbers: the whole atmosphere of the place. He forgot his family in the prisons of Bordeaux, he forgot the ruined home; he suddenly recalled his clear enthusiasms of two years before, when he had saluted the new Liberty as a boy and had thrown himself largely into the current of the New World and let it sweep him along: and he spoke extremely well.

It was a speech worthy of the Gironde, modu-lated in the deep and rising tones which the great river was to make famous in Paris, but more ardent and more convinced in its creed than anything the Parliament men of the Gironde had given or could give. It was almost as though the battalion from Marseilles, the volun-teers who had just done the work and stormed the palace, had found a voice as the young man threw himself into the ardour of that charge.

The Brethren stared at him, three hundred fixed pairs of eyes: the Executive wondered what manner of Jacobin this Bordeaux Jacobin might be; they envied the advantages of his uniform, and his sword, and his youth. Later, men remembering that speech, wondered whether

Saint-Just had not perhaps come among them in disguise. His vision of the society that was to be had nearly carried Boutroux beyond his purpose, but he remembered to present that purpose as he closed.

The flame of his speech died down to a hot ember; he let his voice sink and yet gather clarity when he told them of what had happened in his native city.

For some minutes he detailed to them, point by point, picking one from the other with the gestures of his hands, the plot against the patriots, hatched in old Boutroux's house; the butchery of the common people that was just discovered in time, and just failed; how its failure was only just accomplished by the news of the popular success in Paris. He had not been in the Jacobins of Bordeaux for nothing, this young man from Chiersac, and all he said was a hammered gospel to his hearers.

Old Boutroux, he told them (and they believed it), was a fool. If they made him suffer for what had happened they would but be doing what so many of the societies had done — an injustice, and a wasted injustice, upon the wrong man. They had best let him go after fining him for the purposes of the nation . . . and let them bleed him well, he said, for the firm could stand it. Madame Boutroux could no more conspire than could an old hen: they would be wise and merciful and humorous in letting her go free. Many laughed and applauded as he spoke thus generously of his enemies.

"But," he added, "there were others. . . . First"—he raised his hand to deprecate a possible interruption—"whether they would believe it or no, the President of the Society of Bordeaux was the least trustworthy of men. He had taken money from young Boutroux; there were witnesses to prove it. He named the witnesses, and as he did so he saw the ostler gravely nodding. "That President," he said, "must be destroyed."

The general movement that ran through the crowd as he said this was one of surprise and of awe, but not of contradiction.

"There are witnesses," he said again, and he told their names again. "I am telling you no untrue thing. The money was paid—a whole thousand livres on the very night of the plot." He was there and he had seen the thing done. "Next as to Boutroux himself," and as he mentioned the traitor's name his eyes grew stern.

"That man," he said, "I can discover to you, and if you are wise you will advise those of our Society who are so deputed to approach him without warning and to take a full vengeance. He is even now in my step-mother's house." He hesitated a moment. "Do the brethren think I lack in filial virtue since I so love the State?"

The three hundred of them shouted, "No!"

"Then I will be a Brutus and pursue my duty to the end. Were she my own mother," he added, with a catch in his voice, "I could not bear to do it, but she is not. She married my father," his voice solemnly fell, "when I was a child; she devoured his substance; he died cursing her with his latest breath; she has been nothing but evil to me and to my commune and to the poor. And as such vile things will, within her small measure she would deliberately betray the State."

The audience sat with their mouths open.

"She was a go-between; she took in the letters that came secretly from the Tyrant's friends; she helped the escape of the traitors from this very regiment in which I serve. I tell you she was the soul of treason in all that part, and you must deal with her and hers according to it. And as to the man himself," he concluded, his voice alive with hatred, "he sits in that house dressed in my clothes, calling himself her son, taking my name of Perrin—my father's name—and thinks himself secure. Hawks of the People! fall suddenly upon that nest and tear it!"

And having said this Boutroux had done.

Never since the Society had been formed in Poitiers had the Brethren had anything to do but talk. Now, when first they had to act, what a godsend was here in this young soldier! They pressed round him when his speech was done; some of the elder men took and would not loose his hands; they told him that he was of the kind that saved a State; that he was a Leader! that he should suffer nothing for his boldness.

When he was free from his admirers, the Executive, still jealous of so much power proceeding from a stranger, and a speech that would eclipse all their own, took down his exact instructions: where the house was to be found, at what hours the man might best be caught, how he would affect his alias and call paid witnesses (they all knew the wealth of the Boutroux) to swear to him, while he, Sergeant Perrin, the true heir of that household, was slaving away as a soldier and perhaps lying dead in the cause of the People.

Having so concluded his business, Boutroux went out. The ostler, who had treated him with not too much respect some hours before, was looking at him now almost with dread. He begged to accompany him back to barracks.

"If you will," said Boutroux.

"The deputation will start to-morrow," he said, "by the coach for Angoulême and Bordeaux, and I shall be upon it."

"Well," said Boutroux simply, "do your duty!"

"The young man shall have his due," said the ostler ominously.

"It is well," said Boutroux simply again, "and let the old woman have it also. But that other traitor in Bordeaux who was President, surely you can deal with him also summarily?"

"We shall see," said the ostler. "He is President of a Society and must speak for himself, but Boutroux we will destroy," and they parted at the barrack gates.

Even as he came in, at the guard there were orders and a lieutenant waiting unexpectedly.

Boutroux saluted and showed his night-leave.

"That's all right," said the lieutenant, impatiently glancing at it; "are you not from Chiersac?"

Thought Boutroux to himself, "How curiously these things group themselves! . . . Yes, my Lieutenant," he answered aloud.

"The authorities would speak to you," said the other, nodding at the orderly room. "They are from the police, and they have just come."

"Anything I can do," said Boutroux grimly. He went into the orderly room and found there an official of Bordeaux with his legal secretary. They were apologetic; they would not detain him; they had no great business with him; but was he not from Chiersac? They were on the track of a common murderer who had escaped through that district. A man nick-named Miltiades had been murdered in Bordeaux, and the murderer had got off next morning. He had been traced to Chiersac. They had heard that Sergeant Perrin had enlisted from near by. Could he inform justice?

Sergeant Perrin could not at first recall the murder; but as the details were given him he got it clearer, and he began to nod emphatically.

"Yes," he said, "I heard the whole story; I heard it from a man of Blaye. But," he added, a little confusedly, "I feel it rather treasonable to tell you."

"You'd better tell all you know," said the lawyer, while the official pulled out a little book for his notes and sharpened his pencil.

"Oh, I'm not bound in any way," said Boutroux shamefacedly, "but I think an old man at Blaye must have known more than he cared to say, for when the people in the inn there pressed him he grew silent and sulky, and at last he went out."

"The name of that witness?" murmured the lawyer, ready to take it down.

"I don't know his name," said Boutroux frankly; "I know he was from Blaye, because he said so and everybody else talked of him as coming from that place. I can describe him to you."

"Go on," said the lawyer.

Then did Boutroux very carefully and minutely describe the old man of the ox-cart. When he had done he said significantly, "If you cannot get a clue from him, I doubt if you can get it from any one."

"Will you be prepared to give depositions?" asked the lawyer.

"Well, I'm with the army," said Boutroux.

"But we may take your signed and sworn evidence when we have got the old man?"

"Certainly," said Boutroux, "certainly. I will do all I can to help."

They thanked him, and he was dismissed.

"It is a pity," said Boutroux to himself by way of prayers that night as he fell asleep, "that one cannot do the right thing without involving so many other people beside one's self. But what would you have?" he thought, as he gave his last deep sigh before slumber. "One's own good is almost always some one else's bane. And God knows I have never hurt any that acted justly by me."

With which meditation he fell into a very healthy and contented sleep, and woke from it in the first hours just before dawn to the clangour of the trumpets and the rumour of all the quarters for the march.

CHAPTER XVII.

In which an Old Gentleman shows the Way to an Old Lady.

THE regiment marched day upon day, a long train of straggling horses in the late summer weather; the new recruits were drilled evening after evening in the market-squares of the little towns.

Twice, at Loches and at Blois, there were desertions; and in the early mornings, after summary courts, firing platoons and the shooting of men.

At Blois, also, a few more recruits came in, too late, one would have thought, to be used—but in those days everything was used. The remounts were dragged from the stables of peasants, by force and under order of the Government, as they went along, not without squabbles, nor, once or twice, without bloodshed.

They reached Orleans, and stayed for forty-

eight hours in the cavalry barracks of the town.
The dull place was even fuller of rumour than
had been Poitiers; the breath of Paris was upon
it, and the colonel was anxious to be away, for
even in that short delay he lost ten men, and he
dared not recover them as he might have done
further down country. They left Orleans before
dawn for Chateauneuf, a short day, and one
undertaken only to get away from the constriction
of the populace and the Clubs and the turmoil
of a great town that ruined the order of the
regiment. But at Chateauneuf the rumour spread
among the men that the march would now be
direct for the frontier, and even in the little
villages of the valley the news from the frontier
had come: the armies of the kings were over the
frontier; the invaders were on the soil of the
Nation—and Verdun had fallen.

Soldiers are not concerned with news; but in
the minds of soldiers, even though they be
soldiers but recently civilian, every soldierly place
and stronghold has a meaning. For armies have
a sort of consciousness running through them:
the chance words of officers overheard by their
servants, the politicians of the barrack room
discussing affairs, a mere vague comprehension
of the map—all this inhabits the mind of the men

whose trade it is to go forward by the great roads to battle, and whose nourishment is the open air.

Verdun had fallen; and the little town and the hussars that had just ridden in were abuzz with the news.

Late that night, when, with half a dozen of the sergeants who had midnight leave, Boutroux sat, wearied to death, in a tiny inn, he heard opinion on fire. The men from the street mixed with the soldiery, and one man urged another on to violence. As he so sat—it was past ten o'clock, and he was about to sacrifice his leave and sleep— a man came in from quarters with an order. The regiment was pressed to march, and the sergeants were sent for.

They rose, grumbling; they found in quarters the lights and the movement of a disturbed evening and of sudden commands. A captain, tall, and cloaked against the night, stood at the gate of the guard checking a paper in his hand which one of the men on guard lit from a lantern held above it. He murmured names and the business of each to his non-commissioned officers; one after another saluted and went off about the thing he was bidden to do. The captain's pencil zig-zagged down the sheet, scratching out this, adding that. He came to the name Perrin.

"Sergeant Perrin," he said.

Boutroux saluted.

"I think you are trustworthy?"

"I hope so," said Boutroux.

"My lad," said the captain in a totally different tone—as he looked up under the lantern light Boutroux saw the face of one long broken to the service—"when you have been in the career as long as I have, you will learn never to answer a superior."

The refrain sounded familiar, and Boutroux saluted again.

"Sergeant Perrin," continued the captain, falling again into the kindly and simple tone of a man who is ordering something very difficult, "you will get five horses from a house which is marked suspect." He fumbled a little with his paper, peered at it closely with his keen eyes, and added, "The Spinster de La Roche. Dismiss!"

Then it was that Boutroux wished one were allowed to ask questions in the service; but he knew better by now, and with the ridiculous stiff movement which the service requires, he turned sharply round and walked away. The captain called after him,—

"You will take five men."

He turned round stiffly again from about

thirty yards away, saluted, and said, "Yes, my Captain."

He went back to the barrack room, took five men at random ; one of them had been his equal as a recruit in the first days of the march and pretended to familiarity with him ; he silenced the man, made the five fall in with this old comrade as a sort of corporal to embrigade them, and marched out of quarters into the night.

The street was empty ; there were no lights ; he had no conception of where the Spinster de La Roche might live, still less did he know how he would be received.

"The service," thought Boutroux, "makes of men naturally polite a very nasty set of beings."

He knocked at a door at random : there was no answer. He bade the men force it, and it was forced. From the top of the rude stair within came first a grumble as of a man half awake ; there was the clicking of a tinder-box being struck ; at last a light glimmered, and an old man of surprising energy put his head over a landing above and cursed them for a cartload of devils, asking whether he lived in a free country or not, and whether it was thus that a citizen should be disturbed at midnight, and who was safe when such things could be. To whom Boutroux called up sharply,—

"You are required to give us direction to the house of the Spinster de La Roche, and, if necessary, to lead us there."

"If necessary, to lead you there!" snarled the old man in his nightgown, holding the candle high above his head: "if necessary, to lead you there! I'll lead you to hell first!"

"No," said Boutroux, "you will do that just afterwards."

For a moment it seemed that the old man would give trouble: he was on the point of turning from them, and Boutroux foresaw questions in quarters and a very bad time next morning. But the citizen thought better of it. He reappeared with peasant trousers slipped over his legs, a rough coat upon his shoulders, still wearing his nightgown by way of a shirt, and his absurd cotton nightcap by way of a hat, and so came down.

"You can find it for yourself," he grumbled. "if you will follow my instructions — the woman's known enough in all conscience!" Then he chuckled.

"If your instructions are clear, Citizen," said Boutroux, "you need not come."

The old man was a little mollified by that. He was weak upon the grades of an army; he did not understand the stripes.

"Captain," he said more humbly—and the private soldier leading the others grinned—"I am willing enough to come, but you understand one lives in the same town, and though the lady's reputation . . ."

"Oh yes, I understand," said Boutroux; "but where is it?"

"I'll come with you," sighed the old fellow. He fetched a ramshackle lantern, wasting an intolerable time about it, and came hobbling back with it. "Now," he said, "let us go out. It is not half a mile."

They left the town; they passed along a sandy lane through a little wood to the north of it; they came to a high wall, pierced by a green wooden door; the door was moss-grown and dilapidated.

"The Château is through there," said the old man.

"The Château!" said Boutroux.

"She is a person of consequence," said the old man. "I have no quarrels; I am no politician; I live and let live. She is a person of consequence . . of the rest I say nothing. And let me tell you, from what I know of the old cat, she dislikes to be disturbed, and her doors are always locked."

"Doors give way so easily," said Boutroux, "and it's always work for the locksmith." He beckoned two men forward. Their shoulders took the old green door : it did not open, but the rotten wood of it broke, and they forced their way through into a venerable and dilapidated garden. A grass-grown path, once gravelled, was before them ; the lantern light shone high into the thick foliage of ancient trees.

"I need not go further, Major ?" said the old man anxiously.

"Up to the house !" said Boutroux firmly, "up to the house ! You must remember we are strangers here and need an introduction."

The old man went up to Boutroux's side and spoke in a low voice, that he might not be overheard by the men.

"You will be kind to me," he whispered "Colonel ? After all, we have to live and let live : it is a small town."

"Come along, Citizen," said Boutroux, "come along !"—and the old man came along.

In fifty yards they were at the moat of the old great place. It stood awfully tall and sombre in the night, like a huge square tower with its high

ate roofs, solemn chimneys of two hundred years
mong the stars ; the big doors were shut fast,
ıt a light glimmered within, and through the
ass above the entry they could see the reflection
' that light upon a carved and ancient ceiling.
'utside these closed doors swung a great bell.
hey would not have found its chain in the
ırkness, but the old man showed them where
» find it. Boutroux pulled it, and its loud
angour rang through the park and the trees,
ıd woke echoes within the old house itself.
'here was a shuffling of feet within, and (how
reminded him of home !) a little square wicket,
-ated, pierced in the door, was opened cautiously.
'hey were asked their business.

Boutroux gave it. "The hussars," he said.
We are sent on requisition."

A quavering woman's voice answered,—

"I have orders to admit no one."

"Tell your mistress," said Boutroux, with his
ye to the little iron opening, and seeing within a
nall, thin, trembling woman, white-haired and
ıpped in the manner of the district, "tell your
ıistress that we are here to do no harm—but there
urgent business from the Army."

She bade him wait. She kept them waiting
ıere a good quarter of an hour, and when she

10

came back said, as pompously as her thin cracke
voice would allow,—

"My lady will receive you."

"Give her my best regards," said Boutrou
"and bid her have no fear at all. It is th
business of the Nation."

The great doors were opened, creaking; th
light from within poured upon the park.

The old man said anxiously, whispering agai
"Need I stay?"

"No, Citizen," said Boutroux, "you are fre
of these things."

"You will not give my name to her? She ha
many friends—too many!" said the man anxiously

"I would, of course, betray your name if
knew it," said Boutroux doubtfully; "but I d
not know it. However, I will guess at it."

The old man eyed him misunderstandingly, an
made off. He had no love for the politics of h
time, and as he went back through the darkness t
his disturbed repose he loved them less than ever

"The world," said he to himself, "is comin
to an end . . . so it was foretold . . . so it wa
foretold. Old Stephen's niece, whom he force
to be a nun in Orleans, foretold it. . . . She wa
right, it is the end of the world!" And s
muttering, he went back homewards.

CHAPTER XVIII.

In which an Old Lady shows the Way to a Young Gentleman.

BOUTROUX entered the hall out of the night with his five men. He heard behind him joke that did not please him, and he turned und sharply.

"*Fixe !*" he shouted.

They shuffled into a sort of line ; he bade them ut up their arms and take their places upon the k bench with its fine carved end, that ran ong the stone wall.

"If anything goes amiss to-night, I shall make the worse for you," he said ; and as he said it, he oked at the man who had presumed upon his cient comradeship, and the man was afraid.

As he turned round from saying this, he saw ming towards him the mistress of the place, and e heard a very pleasant, gentle, somewhat ironical oice saying to him,—

"To what do I owe your visit, Lieutenant?"

"The number of ranks," thought Boutrou[x] "through which a man may pass in time of revol[u]tion and of war is infinite! . . . Madame," answered her aloud, "it is a very small matt[er] Five horses were requisitioned, and they have n[ot] come."

"They were requisitioned, Lieutenant," said t[he] lady, speaking like fine metal, like silver temper[ed] to steel, "a month ago. I have since held the[m] ready; no one has asked for them . . . and now y[ou] come for them at midnight and in arms!"

Boutroux, standing straight, with his sword [in] its scabbard, respectfully held and low, as might [be] that of a gentleman with some message to gi[ve] took her in. He remembered the term "suspect[ed]" in his orders, and he watched her well.

She was not tall nor large in body, and yet s[he] was not frail : there was something of self-posse[s]sion, if not in her soul, at least in her carriage, a[nd] a pretty dignity of movement. She was dress[ed] all in black, with white lace at her throat and h[er] wrists; her hands, he thought as he watched he[r] were singularly small and strong. They we[re] clasped before her. Her hair was grey, wi[th] touches of a whiter grey in it; it was her ow[n] hair. Her face still wore that light ironic smil[e]

d her eyes were very pleasing : they were black,
d they had in them, as she watched him, an
pression which provoked him not a little to
ow more of her.

"Madame, I have no written order," said
outroux, seriously moved. "I intend no dis-
urtesy—but the Army is in urgent need. If I
d a written order it would be easier."

"There is no need for that, Lieutenant," she
swered in a lower tone, and with a charm-
g submission. "The Army may do what it
ills."

"But I will give you the receipt and the claim,
d all that you may ask for verification," con-
nued Boutroux eagerly. "I really regret, I very
eatly regret . . ."

"You need not regret, Lieutenant," she said.
We must all do our duty. And now let me
ll you. . . . But wait a moment : I will call a
an."

She left the hall : her light steps sounded fainter
nd fainter as she traversed the house to her
ffices. She came back with one of her grooms,
w-browed, solemn, and resentful.

"Louis," she said, "you will accompany these
entlemen : they have come for West Wind,
ericles, Queen, Furtive, and Basilisk."

The groom touched his head. "Basilisk can
go out, my lady," he said.

"Why not ?" she asked.

"He's lame, my lady," said the groom.

"Is it bad, Louis ? Does it prevent his work
ing ?"

"Yes, my lady," said the man more stubborn
than ever.

"Why, all the better," said she cheerfully, th
unexpected lady of the night. "I could wish the
all had such a complaint. I could wish they ha
each but three legs a-piece," and she smiled :
Boutroux, who gravely and slightly smiled i
return. "Horses which are needed by the Natio
Lieutenant, are at the disposal of the Nation : an
these are the five that were requisitioned, nam
for name. I regret that one of them should b
lame."

"Madame," answered Boutroux solemnly, "
have had stiff legs in the saddle myself, but I hav
not been excused from marching."

"Louis," said the lady, turning to the groom
"take these gentlemen with you." She pointe
to the five soldiers. "Do you requisition saddle
also, Lieutenant ?"

"Well, Madame," said Boutroux, "it is not i
my orders, but I confess that horses withou

saddles, though the easier to ride, are impossible
for the service. There is this and that and the
rest . . ."

"But you cannot expect me to have campaign
saddles ?" she said.

"Madame," he said, "no doubt we shall find
them when we join the main body."

"No doubt," she said, "no doubt. . . . Come,
Louis, take these gentlemen away !"

The groom, with the worst of wills, led off the
lumpish soldiers.

"And you, sir," she said, turning to Boutroux,
"pray come in and take wine : it will not be a
short business, only two of the horses are in the
stable here. Two others are at the farm at the
end of the park, and one will have to be caught.
He is out at grass."

"I am at your orders, Madame," said Boutroux.

She led him through two great *pièces* where
tapestry hung, and of which the floors were of
uneven chestnut, glazed to a polish by many
generations of coming and going. In one of these,
which was her dining-room, she picked up a flask
of wine and a glass for him. She stooped to find
bread in a sideboard : it was too low for her, and
he went down upon one knee.

Said Boutroux to himself : " What queens one finds upon the march ! "

She brought out the bread and the flask ; he took them from her.

" Really, Madame," he said, " I cannot allow . . .

" Oh, be silent ! " said the lady lightly, " we know the Army here ! " And then she added " Lieutenant—Verdun has fallen ! "

" Yes," said Boutroux, to whom that news was of no great weight at such a moment.

They went together into a little room through the door, a room with a tall ebony bookcase in it, a little marble chimney-piece, and the conventional sham gold clock of the time, with a looking-glass behind it. The little room was full of the scent of late roses, of which a glorious group stood in a jar upon her table. Upon that table also there was a book laid open, as though she had but just left reading it. He did not see the title of the book, and he wondered what it might be. Two candles stood upon that table, still and unflickering in the dark summer air. Their light shone on a terrace without.

" The night is warm, Lieutenant ; we will take this wine for you, and this bread, outside and put them upon a little iron table that is there, and sit there until your men have returned."

Boutroux was willing enough. She followed him out to the terrace, and as she followed she blew the candles out.

That small enclosed park was fragrant in the August night—it was secluded. One might dream in it, in such a night, that there were no such things as grooming and marching and arms.

There came from time to time a country noise from the distant village, the sharp bark of a dog, or the lowing of a beast in a stable : the faintest and most distant of those sounds could be heard through the clear summer air ; and above them, shining through warm heaven, was a wilderness of stars.

"Lieutenant," said the lady, "are you for the frontier ? "

"Yes, Madame," he said, "and all the regiment."

For a few moments she kept silence, and then she said,—

"I envy you, Lieutenant."

"It is plain truth, Madame," he said, "that people told me your house was suspect ; but I do assure you, by my lack of a beard, that I will keep faith with anything you say, for I am neither with one set of the dogs nor with the other."

She laughed gently in the darkness.

"When you are my age, Lieutenant," she said,

"you will be more certain of that than ever, and you will only take sides in the things to which your heart moves you. . . . No, the house is not suspect . . . but I regret the better times." She drew her shoulders together ; he could just see the movement : he thought she was cold, in spite of the warmth of the hour, or that she felt the dampness of the moat. He went in without her bidding, fumbled in the dark room, and at last brought out through the open window a shawl that he had noticed cast across the arm of a chair ; he put it round her, not hastily.

"I have heard," thought Boutroux to himself as he lingered upon this gesture, "that a woman is not a woman until she is forty : now this lady is certainly a woman."

She thanked him, and she said,—

"Lieutenant . . .? When do you march ?"

"I do not know, Madame ; too soon, whatever the hour may be."

"But to-morrow ?" she said.

"Yes, certainly, Madame, and more probably this very night."

"You soldiers never sleep," she replied to him, in such a tone of pity that he was moved again.

"But when we sleep, Madame, we sleep sound.'

"Yes," she said, "you sleep sound."

He wondered what the Army was to her, and why she spoke so of the Army. She went on,—

"Lieutenant, will you do me a favour?"

"Madame," said Boutroux with singular alertness, "I will do you any favour that is within my power, and most of those that are not."

"You have spoken as a man of the trade should," she answered nobly. "Do you know, Lieutenant, we women who stay behind love men who will do what is asked of them by the Nation . . . or by any other dame."

"Aye, Madame," he said, "and we soldiers love to be asked it . . ."

She asked what he did not expect.

"Why then, Lieutenant, tell me, I pray you, while those clodhoppers are stealing my cattle, tell me how you came to be in the service, and to be marching thus. Had you ever the King's commission?"

His eyes were used to the darkness, the haunting light of the summer stars glimmered upon the gracious curves of her grey and silvering hair, but her eyes were quite in shadow. Her face was turned towards him, and he could imagine many things.

"I will tell you the truth," he said gravely,

pausing a little before he answered, "I never held a commission of the King's."

"Then why are you here?" she said. "Was it the invasion that stirred you?"

"No, Madame," said Boutroux more gravely still, "not even the invasion, though I trust I should have done my duty. Shall I tell you the whole story?"

"Why," she said, with a little laugh, "that is just what I have asked you to do."

Boutroux let his head fall back in the darkness and stared up at the great stars.

"I am by birth," he said slowly, and thinking at large, "I am by birth the son of a lawyer in Paris, a Judge of the High Court. My father was, and is, the kindest and tenderest of fathers. He designed me in marriage—it was before the troubles, Madame; it was before these worries that I hate, and do not understand—he designed me in marriage for a young lady against whom I have nothing to say. She had every grace and quality and charm, and a dowry, as I was given to believe, of three hundred thousand livres."

"It is a large sum," said the lady gently.

"It is a large sum, Madame," agreed Boutroux, shrugging his shoulders, "but it was destined never to be mine."

"Indeed! Pray tell me more, for I am interested."

"It is a simple story, Madame." He drew a deep breath, which is a kind of inspiration, and continued,—

"The lady who brought me up, you must know, was neither a nurse nor a governess, but something between the two. With her daughter I played as a sister, and we grew up together."

"Boy," said the lady here, "I see what is coming."

"Ah, Madame," said Boutroux, "then you are far wiser than I. . . . She died."

"She died?" said the lady, surprised.

"Yes," said Boutroux, leaning forward, and holding his scabbard between his knees, and letting his voice sink profoundly, "she died: a purer, nobler, more. . . ."

"Yes, yes," said the lady. (Far off at the end of the little park lights were coming, and time was short.) "I understand," she ended rapidly.

"You understand, Madame," said Boutroux with a sob.

"And so you are here?"

"And so I am here!" said Boutroux simply.

"Did you enlist, since you say you have not the King's commission?"

"I enlisted, Madame; I enlisted at St. Denis at the cavalry depot. I was in the ranks for two years."

The lady leaned towards him, and consented to put a hand for one moment upon his hand. Boutroux was willing; no movement of his condemned the gesture. The lights from the end of the park were approaching, and they could just begin to hear the loud banter of the five soldiers quizzing the groom.

"Men do not often rise as you have risen," she said. "Tell me before we part how you obtained your grade."

"It is a curious story, Madame. An old gentleman whose name I did not know, but who had evidently great authority, was for promoting me with an indecent rapidity. I had already been named a sergeant for some weeks, when he urged me successively up the ranks of lieutenant, captain, major, and even colonel."

"It is incredible!" said the lady, staring at him with wide eyes.

"Yes, Madame, incredible, and, as I thought at the time, ill-judged, and even ignorant; but so it was. I paid but little attention to his patronage; I did not believe that he had any real power. What gave me my commission, and that to which I owe my lieutenancy, was the very generous act of a woman."

"Really, Lieutenant," said the lady, "women seem to have played a part in your life!"

"Ah, Madame," said Boutroux solemnly, "I never knew how much until to-night."

"And so," went on the lady, a little too rapidly, "it is to a woman that you owe your title of lieutenant, you very young man?"

"It is, Madame," said Boutroux.

"Did she know you well?"

"No, Madame, nor I her; but for a brief moment upon a summer night I loved her well enough."

"What power had she to give you such advancement?"

"Nothing, Madame, but her word; yet her words were of a sort and spoken in a tone which I will long remember."

The horses moving up the drive, their pace upon the stones of it, the men leading them, and the grumbling of the groom, were now close at hand. She rose unwillingly.

They went into the darkened room together, and as she passed before him through the open windows she said, in the lowest of voices but one as clearly heard as a summons, "We are in no haste to join the others." It was some little time before either spoke again. When that silence broke, she broke it first in a changed voice, still holding him in the darkness.

"You march before dawn?" she asked.

"Madame," he said, standing before her in the night, "I have told you : we go when we are ordered, and I believe that the orders will come by daybreak or before."

"Well," she said, catching at her words, "I shall ask from you a receipt . . . and a due note . . . I can give you nothing more in exchange."

She lit the candles again in that little room ; he seemed to remember a room which he had known, not for a few moments, but for some days. She wrote in a delicate and clear hand the note of the horses' names, the description which she had afforded of them to the officials, and she put the paper before him to sign. He signed it. Neither had looked at the other's eyes. She sanded the ink and dried it ; she folded the paper with his signature upon it, and put it into her bosom.

"And now," she said, "Lieutenant, Lieutenant, I can give you nothing more ! "

"Why, Madame," said he, "your good wishes."

"Well, you have had more than that," she whispered, and Boutroux followed her into the hall. . . . Before the great door of it were the five horses and the men, and the groom standing sullen ; they had waited too long.

Boutroux once outside her door, and standing at a horse's head, turned to the lady of the house as she stood with the light upon her watching him go. "Have I your leave to mount ?" he said.

"All my leave to all you will," she answered.

"Then," said Boutroux to the groom, "which horse did you say was lame ?"

But the groom muttered : "I take no orders from you."

One of his men said, "This one, Sergeant," leading up a brown mare of no capacity. Boutroux took the stirrup iron in his right hand, and measured the stirrup leather against his left arm. "It is my length," he said, and he mounted. With the first movement of his mount he thought, "No more lame than I—less ! " He drew his sword and saluted as he left that house, then he sheathed it again.

"Louis," said the lady—it was the last time he heard her voice—" show the lieutenant to the great gate and bid them open it. Lead the lieutenant ! " she added sharply.

"Sergeant!" muttered the groom to himself.

The doors shut again upon her, and the little troop went up to the great stone pillars and the wrought-iron gate, where a light in the lodge was already awaiting them, and some figure was moving in the darkness to open.

Riding behind his men Boutroux could not forbear to look over his shoulder ; he saw, or thought he saw, near a light upon the first story the head, and the inclination of the body, and the gesture with which an hour's acquaintance had too much accustomed him. But he turned and went through the gate, and he said to the groom as he did so,—

"When they press you for the wars, my man, try to be under my command ; and if I am colonel by that time—for my promotion is rapid—I will see that you have an easy time—in prison."

The man answered him with a fine curse, and they parted.

CHAPTER XIX.

In which it Rains.

IT was broad daylight of the next morning when the long column of cavalry on its eastward way out from Chateauneuf filed along the highroad past those same gates again.

Boutroux saw the wrought-iron gates and the stone pillars, which had stood so strangely out under the lanterns in the night, now much older under the freshness of the new day; dead leaves were beginning to fall from the avenue of trees, for that tragic autumn had come early; the statued edge of the moat, and the ancient house behind it, carried upon them in the daylight every mark of decay.

The shutters of it were closed fast; there was moss, and here and there a growth of yellow flowers upon the stonework of the walls. It was but a glimpse down the avenue as the regiment trotted past; in a moment the trees and the high park wall had cut off the sight. But in that moment there occurred to the young man's mind a phrase : that things differ within and without, and that what they seem at night they seem not in the morning. He carried the phrase and the picture of that deserted and ancient place ; he carried it within him for miles of hard going.

From that day the march proceeded with an increased anxiety about it and an increased haste : the work was harder night after night, the leisure less, the tests for sickness or for leave more severe. And still as they went eastward they came nearer to the flavour of the war.

The emptiness of the land after the harvest, the stubble and the lack of men in the fields, increased that impression of doom. September was entered, the first week of it was half gone ; they were still urged forward.

The men understood nothing of all this save that the crisis had come, and that these pressed marches, the saddle sores, the horses left behind, the remounts of every sort and kind, the haste and anarchy of the whole business, was a race to join the front.

Such of them as could form some idea of the map of the country understood where the

Boutroux rode by the side of his wretched lot. He communed with his old white horse Pascal, and called it his friend, and begged it to be cheered. He bade it note that never was a thing so bad but soon it would probably be worse. He conjured it in the name of their fast friendship not to fall down in that night and die.

Pascal went forward ; the rain streamed down the soaked hair of his scraggy neck. He had his fill of soldiering. His poor horse-soul was ready for the end.

Hamard the lieutenant was in command of that troop : captain they had none. The young officer knew the ranks and how to deal with them : he was not six weeks commissioned, it was not two years since he had groomed his own horse as a private, and of such stuff the best subaltern command in these armies was made. The open complaints of the men were nothing to him ; he left the rough to his sergeant. Boutroux did the work with his own few, cursing and jeering by turns, over-looking, accountable for his number. There was the worst of example around.

In the troop before them was disorder. One young fellow of a brutish sort had let his jaded mount fall in the later hours of that bad night ;

he had stepped out of the saddle as one might step out of a chair, and had said,—

"The beast will die there, and I shall lie down too"—saying which he had thrown himself at full length upon the mud by the roadside, and no one had disturbed him : the regiment rode on.

Another, half an hour later, took the occasion of a driving gust which blinded them all, to veer off as they passed through trees and to be lost to the service. It was three in the morning when the miserable column, not seven hundred sabres, huddled into the town of St. Dizier, through which they had passed fifteen hours before on their way eastward at noon ; there at last they were told by sections that they might rest.

The foragers had gone before ; the houses were numbered in which the few privileged might sleep, and the barns in which the many must throw themselves, drenched as they were, upon the straw. There was no provision. A butcher's shop, with the iron shutters tight fastened, and the gilded ox's head which was its sign dripping rain in the darkness, stood upon the street where Boutroux's troop were gathered huddled, a-foot, holding their unhappy beasts in the pouring darkness, and waiting for the appointment to shelter.

Boutroux, not yet dismounted, went up to the lieutenant and said : "My Lieutenant, the men must eat."

The officer answered : "I have not eaten."

"My Lieutenant," said Boutroux, "may I ask the people in this house for food?"

"It is my place," said the lieutenant.

All ranks were confused, and all order and discipline in peril, save that a score of bedraggled and wretched men in their utter fatigue looked upon these two for succour.

Boutroux struck heavily at the door of the house; there was no answer, and the only noise he heard when the echo of his scabbard against the wood had died was the sedulous drumming of the rain. He dismounted, holding his own horse, led it, and going himself close to the door, at the length of his bridle he charged it with the full strength of his shoulder; it broke open, and a tiny night light showed a flight of dirty stairs and a gaping passage-way within.

The lieutenant held out his hand and took Boutroux's bridle to leave him free. He said "Thank you, my Lieutenant," and went within.

Those who dwelt in the house above lay low;

they either did not hear or would not hear. Boutroux picked up a piece of paper that lay greasy and long upon the foul steps, twisted it, lit it at the night light, and held it above his head in the shop. A great piece of meat hung with twenty others upon their hooks near to hand ; it was heavy and he was very weak with the march and fasting ; he slung it off somehow and staggered with it outside. The men, who saw him in the darkness and under the rain carrying some burden, smelled and knew that it was meat. Two of them laughed, and another called out to him with praise and affection, calling him by the nickname that his men had chosen.

The little pack of them went off to a barn near by, took the dry straw, made a clear space upon the flags so that the fire should not catch ; they lit the straw, they broke off projecting ends of planks and weather boardings, and one way and another they made a smoky fire. The poor beasts that had carried them were tied up as best they could be, to the rings and pillars of the high dark place : outside the rain fell soddenly.

One man had found a lantern and had lit it. No one concerned himself for guard or sentry, but Boutroux and the lieutenant saw to it that before anything else was done, two men should take pails that were there and find water, which they did from the pump of the market square, and taking it in turns, and each as he was so ordered, upon the point of rebellion, they came back and forth until all the horses were watered. Until this was done the men might not eat. There was no corn under that great wooden roof, but there was a little scattered hay which was seized for the horses, and straw in abundance; this also they ate eagerly. Boutroux came round in the darkness to his old beast Pascal, where its white coat glimmered like a long ghost in a corner of the barn. He told it that things of this sort lasted but a little time for horse or man; he hoped his horse was as proud as he was to serve the State, and he stroked its nose to cheer it. He thought he felt the foolish brute lean its head towards him for companionship.

Before the fire Boutroux could smell the toasting of the meat upon jack-knives and bits of pointed wood sharpened for spits. One of the men, under some influence of habit, had asked the lieutenant to distribute the rations. There was plenty for all. Not a few in their desperate need were sucking the raw meat before they toasted it, and no one asked for bread. But in an extreme thirst several plunged their faces into the buckets from which the horses had drunk, full of the slime of them, and drank as beasts drink. . . . And that is the way in which twenty of the regiment passed the night in St. Dizier in mid-September of 1792.

A cannon-sound away, not more, the great army of the invaders had forced the line of the Argonne hills . . . and these men, in such a plight and under such a discipline, were a grain, a drop, in the many thousands such, who were to attempt battle against Europe—such scenes, such ignorance in the dark, such despair in the rain, are for soldiers the chief part of war.

When they had finished their eating, some upon the raw, some upon the toasted meat, and had lain in their drenched clothes in a stupor for perhaps two hours, a trumpet called, cracked and pitiful, in the street without : daylight had come through the great doors of the barn, and the lieutenant and Boutroux, first rising, aroused their men.

There was no grooming done in that morning ; the steady, drenching pour of the rain outside still broke their hearts ; one man, a young man not long from his cottage in the South, could not move : he moaned to himself, and they left him there, but his horse they took with them, seeing that there were more men than horses left in the last night end of the march. The beasts were given a few more wisps of the hay, a few more broken and cut handfuls of the straw. They were all still serviceable : that is, their lean bodies, their raw sores, their matted and uncleaned coats, had not yet brought them to death ; but as cavalry goes, those hussars were not models of cavalry to see.

All that night only the girths had been loosened, for accoutrement that morning the girths were tightened only. Scabbards and stirrup irons, curb-chains and bridle rings, were a mass of rust as they came out into the daylight. Some of the men were so stiff they could not mount, but had to swing painfully into the saddle from low walls ; others had taken the night more easily, and were ready even to crack jokes in a low tone with their neighbours : as they mounted and proceeded up the main street of St. Dizier, trumpets continued to sound the assembly in cracked and mournful and unfinished notes. The rain still steadily poured, and they set out for their last twenty miles to where, as all the townsfolk told them, Kellermann and his army now did really lie in mass at Vitry.

Such is the life of soldiers that to ride so upon broken beasts in the rain, a straggling mass of hundreds, with no end before them and no knowledge of their goal, yet raised their hearts because through the dull rain it was yet daylight, and the hell of the hours before their sleep had been the dark hours of a hopeless night.

At Longchamp their spirits further rose, for there all the marks of a regular advance were apparent, the chalked numbers were on the doors of the houses and sheds and stables, even the sick who had been left behind were a proof of the great army that lay before ; and best of all, some sort of provision had been organised. They ate and drank human food and drink ; there was wine for the few that could buy it and the many that could steal ; there were detachments of the soldiery already apparent ; there was bread, and, for the first time in how many days, hot coffee in tins.

They left Longchamp by noon for the last stretch of the road, expecting the Army.

At three o'clock in the afternoon the rain ceased, the skies lifted somewhat, the landscape for a few miles could be discerned, and a great town of canvas, the tents of the line, lay apparent

far off upon the sloping flank of a high land
beyond; they heard the distant bugles. They
came to pickets, they saw moving over fields
in the distance large ordered bodies of men,
and when the column halted and was given its
orders for stabling and for quartering, it had
already mixed in spirit and largely in body with
the twenty thousand and more which Kellermann
was leading to join Dumouriez.

Just before those thousands in their drenched
clothes, with their hobbling horses, their limping,
footsore men, their torn and lost accoutrements,
their insufficient and haphazard guns, lay, one
long day's march away, the roll of empty land,
the great marshy plains, where they were called
to meet the strict and brilliant army of the
invasion.

Had any one man seen and appreciated those
two—the huddled regiments at Vitry, and the
noble parade of the successful invasion which
had just turned the line of the Argonne, and
had now nothing between itself and Paris—he
could not for one moment have hesitated in
his decision. If indeed there was material for
contest, that contest would be swiftly decided.
For here was a mob unbroken to the trade, all in
disorder, hopeless with fatigue and lack of food

and sleep and ceaseless rain; and there was the last and the best of the instructed armies of Europe.

But no man so saw the contrast : only Fate.

The men that were thus massed and huddled under Kellermann, after the storms of rain and the mud and the hunger and the death of that marching, were not trusted to accomplish any achievement. They had but to go forward ; and they must perish.

CHAPTER XX.

In which it goes on Raining.

IT was on the 15th of September that the regiment, if it could still be called a regiment at all, so joined the main army.

When the morning of the 16th dawned, the stable guards, the pickets, and the long line of bivouacs in the fields beyond the houses were content to remark that once again it was raining. Far off, up the valley under the rain, a long line of men already moving was Kellermann's advance upon Sampigny, where lay the workshops. No sound yet heard of distant firing reached the hollow of the Marne, no rumours of an enemy's approach ; there was nothing but the rain veiling the landscape, the low sodden hills under it, and the swollen river running turbulent and brown.

With the early morning yet another great bulk of the army broke off for the march on

11

Pogny; but the hussars, and Boutroux with them, had received no orders. The horses were more important than the men, now that they had come to a country too thickly occupied for the gathering of remounts; the beasts were tended therefore, all that morning, under cover, cleaned more or less, and restored after the bad business of the countermarch from Bar-le-Duc and the days and the nights of weather. There was even a trifle of leisure in the force, and men, after the grooming, got into the taverns together, watching the pelt of the rain outside, but at least comforted by wine.

The townsfolk loved the soldiers less and less, and these last comers were given nothing for the sake of their trade. There was a sullen truce and no more between the civilians and the Army.

The noon meal had been eaten; no one had yet seen orders, and even the subalterns in each troop could guess at nothing, when about one o'clock came the news: the regiment saddled, mounted, and began to take an abominable country road northward out of the valley. For all that afternoon it dragged, a long line of men and beasts, over the mud of Champagne, through little plantations of stunted trees, and then again across the bare rolling fields, mile after mile after mile, under the steady fall of the rain.

It was again almost dark, the third day of such an inconvenience, when a tiny hamlet at the edge of a wood appeared before the head of the column, the lights already showing in the windows. A peasant boy was standing out in the downpour huddled under a great blanket, and herding half a hundred sheep. As one of the sergeants who had been sent out to interrogate him approached him, he pounded off in terror: he was caught in a moment, shaken, and dragged back. At first he would not speak; he did not know whether he was dealing with the enemy or with what monstrous forces; but all they wanted of him was the name of the place. It was Cense.

The news reassured the command: the men were glad to perceive in so small a place such great barns for the reception of them and their beasts; and the next day, still under that same weather, leaving behind them twenty men, of whom ten would not see their homes again, the column went forward.

Hamard the lieutenant, riding by Boutroux, said to him suddenly in the middle of that morning, in a gentle ironical voice,—

"Sergeant Perrin, have you studied the art of war?"

"No, sir," said Boutroux.

The lieutenant sighed. "I am sorry for that. Had you studied it in your youth, when, as you tell me, you attended the best classes, you might have told me what we are at, and why we are all alone like this upon filthy country lanes. Short of your information I should have to ask the colonel, and he would put me under arrest, and, when we reached a town, in prison."

"Undoubtedly, sir," said Boutroux with respect.

"Well, but, Sergeant Perrin, since you are an instructed man, pray tell me what all this is."

"I think, sir," said Boutroux grimly, "that we must be a rearguard. I understand that such detachments suffer as we are suffering."

"It is very probable," answered the lieutenant solemnly, and without smiling. "It is a valuable suggestion. If the men need heartening, supposing it still rains to-morrow, I shall let the troop know that we are a rearguard."

The guess was right enough; that afternoon, as the regiment trailed wearily into Fresne, they found all the evidences of a recent passage by a great force. One man showed them the house where Kellermann had slept the night before;

several complained of the sick left behind and quartered upon them. The floor of the town hall was littered with the wastage of such an army upon such a march ; there were dead and dying, lost and broken articles of accoutrement, and a pile of saddles—the saddles of horses which had fallen out and could not be replaced.

The next day the clouds lowered but shed no rain ; the march over the crest to the valley of the Yevre beyond was just more tolerable than the whole past week had been. There was a rising talk in the ranks, and now and then the beginning of a song, and the French laughter could be heard. Even the poor beasts felt the change, and the knowledge of being in touch with the army seemed to put some energy into their going.

At Dommartin, the first town since Vitry, the regiment reposed, entering the place fairly early in the day, and under orders, or the rumours of orders, to rest there for many hours of the next.

And there it was that Boutroux for the first time saw that his mount Pascal, who had carried him so faithfully through such weathers, all these leagues from the centre and from Poitiers, was in a different mood. Pascal, that elderly beast, long ago broken to the necessities of this world, and accustomed in the stable to let his head hang as though in perpetual contemplation of some fate beneath the world, upon this day at Dommartin stood more pathetically and less stolidly despairing ; it had fear in its old eyes, and Boutroux asked the veterinary's orderly to come and see.

The veterinary's orderly came and saw, and said that the horse was fitter to be with God than with men. He squeezed and touched this place and that as his art taught him, the old mount turning round and giving him reproachful looks, and now and then trying to whisk its tail. The veterinary's orderly shook his head.

"Can you get another mount ?" he asked.

"Only by dismounting a man," said Boutroux. "We have done enough of that already."

"Then," said the veterinary's orderly, "ride him till he drops." And with that he went out.

But Boutroux, coming near to his horse and looking at him fondly in the face, said,—

"Horse Pascal, you and I have seen much weather together, and I will call you my constant friend. I have known you for now five weeks, and no other friend I can recall who has been my friend so long, or has remained tolerable at the end of such a space of time. Nor has any friend whom I can recall, and whom I could have wished to stay with me, stayed half so long. I will go and get you something pleasant."

He swaggered round the barn, picking his way in among the legs of the men who were sleeping off their moment of freedom in that afternoon; for no man knew what the night might be. He found upon a shelf at one end of the barn a pile of carrots; he stole three of the largest and came back to the horse.

"Now eat," he said, and the horse bit at the carrots greedily. "Eat, horse, eat: a soldier's life has few pleasures; it is glorious no doubt, but it is weak in pleasures. Eat! A soldier's life is sometimes wet, but now you are in the dry. Eat, my good Pascal; God knows what will come to-morrow."

And even as he said it there were noises in the street without—women's voices shrill and exasperated or in panic, men moving quickly, and immediately afterwards the double sound of the trumpets calling for the heads of troops to come to the colonel.

Boutroux went out: it was the fall of the day; not yet so dark but that a man could read.

The street was full of folk, each giving his version of what had happened ; and from one end of it, the northern end, which leads out towards Auve and the Paris road, numbers came in to swell the crowd.

The enemy had been seen upon the height above Herpont, said one. No, said another, beyond the great road. A third, who said he had seen them himself, and was a liar, swore that the main forces had occupied the line of the great road. A fourth, who was cautious and an atheist by trade, said that these panics came regularly every three days, and that for his part he did not believe a word of it. One of the older sergeant-majors was looking up the street as though expecting something. Boutroux went up to him and asked what the true news was. The old fellow shrugged his shoulders.

"Their cavalry has sent a few scouts forward, that's all."

"How far ?" asked Boutroux.

"No one seems to know," said the old chap.

The captain of the third troop, a man of the recent promotions, rough and full of movement, came up upon his horse, swearing indiscriminately. He called out as he passed that the order was Boot-and-Saddle, and that whoever started first

would have the advantage, for there would be
damned little time after the trumpets.

Boutroux ran back to his own people in the
barn, wakening them, and just as he had done
so the Boot-and-Saddle sounded in the streets
of the little town. But after it, and on the heels
of it, came special orders for haste ; and as the
evening lowered the intolerable business began
again. They were up again, all but the half
dozen or so who had broken down at the end
of this last halt ; some few, lacking mounts from
the collapse of their horses, were left with orders
to follow on foot along the Voilement road.
And as the night fell the regiment was off,
still trailing northward down the valley of the
Yevre.

Why northward or whither, no one but the
command could tell, save that every mile of
the way showed more clearly where the great
army had just passed, and they knew that they
were on the heels of Kellermann. How long
they must march, whether, as most of them
imagined, through the whole night, where they
would come out from their journey, at what place
the junction would be effected, what the chances
of action might be—no one knew. But just when
the darkness was complete, by nine o'clock or so,

11 a

one man and then another felt the coming of a dreadful and familiar thing : it was the rain !

They had had but a day's respite, and it would not leave them now. They bent their shoulders beneath it, and the poor horses their heads, and all night long it fell, cold and continuous, with no wind driving it ; and all night long the column went forward. The going was worse and worse, the mud splashing from the clay lanes thicker and more foul.

It seemed in the small hours to more than one of the men as though something would snap and go, as though such a strain could not be continued. Boutroux, like many another, slumbered in the saddle, jolting on half conscious ; the saddle bags and his stirrups (secretly shortened, against all the traditions of the cavalry) held him in his place.

As he so jolted he thought himself for some moments a postilion before a chaise, upon a dark night in a lonely lane upon an upland ; he felt the rain upon his face. Then he would waken suddenly as the old horse stumbled, or as some neighbour in the darkness banged up against him. Then he would jolt to sleep again, and dream that he was in a cart driving off from the first of his adventures ; and then again he would half

remember in his drowsy head that he was a
soldier and that this was the Army, and he would
wonder how long it might be before they would
reach Poitiers or Bourges, or Orleans or Troyes.
The weeks of marching were fuddled together
in his head as sleep oppressed it. Once and
only once he did completely lose all sense of
motion in the depth of sleep, and then for five
good minutes he dreamt that he smelt the smell
of dried ferns, and that he was well sheltered
in a hiding-place, and that no trouble weighed
on him, because a friend of his would soon come
in and find him there. Of her voice, which in
that moment of dream he clearly remembered,
his mind was still full when he half awoke with
a start that saved his balance. He settled himself into the saddle again, and the remaining
hours of the darkness he still imperfectly, heavily,
and drowsily dreamed.

CHAPTER XXI.

Valmy.

THE day dawned after that night of pitiless rain and mud; the drowned and miserable light, the half-light of the hopeless morning, showed nothing but bare fields in which small stunted trees shivered under the steady drizzle. The column was checked somewhere ahead, the old white horse halted abruptly; Boutroux, lolling in his saddle, was jolted out of his sleep. He straightened himself and was awake.

"The longer I live," he muttered to his wretched mount, "the more I learn! Get up, my poor beast. A man can sleep in the saddle fasting and under a shower-bath. It would astonish them at home!"

As the word crossed his lips he had a sharp vision within him—too sharp, the illusion of fasting and fatigue. He saw the Gironde under the sunlight, the quay, the old and noble houses;

his room and his books returned to him—it was
sleep returning. But the old horse stumbled, and
the picture disappeared. He had a friend and a
reality to hand. Here was a horse who got on
with him well enough. . . . But what a crock !

With that reflection he patted his unfortunate
beast upon its sodden, steaming neck. But the
poor victim was beyond comfort, and put one hoof
before the other mechanically and with weight of
despair.

Boutroux looked round him under the dawn
and saw a miserable sight :

Two miles and more of men stretched straggling along the road before him. In his own troop
there was no semblance of order. The men at his
side and those immediately before him were more
or less his companions, yet not all of the same
troop. Mixed up with them in a hopeless confusion limped a few boys, their uniforms torn, one
of them with a boot cracked to the sole, another
with his face tied up in a chance rag which some
kindly woman had lent him in a farm. He had
the toothache and his cheek was swollen.

Others of the line were jumbled with the
hussars ; two gunners also, come from God knows
where, their dark clothes plastered with mud as
though they had rolled in it, their head-gear too

large for them, squashed down over their ears and
foreheads.

Far ahead a confusion of carts struggled on
through the weather, and in the marshy fields to
the right a ludicrous attempt at a flanking party, a
dozen horses or so, splashed and sucked as best
they could through the drowned clay. Very far off
forward came from time to time a loud, cursing
order; and in one place near by Boutroux could see
a man collapsed upon the roadside, and a sergeant
striking him with the butt end of a musket to
make him move. But the man would not move,
for he was dead. And even as Boutroux saw such
a sight, after all that night and all that fatigue, he
smiled, for in the sight there was something
political; the sergeant was an aged man, and his
regiment was a regiment with traditions, a regiment
that was proud to call itself Artois. The white
facings of it were dingy enough now. The sergeant of Artois abandoned his task, and Boutroux
turned away his eyes. He was not used to the
death of men.

So the dawn rose through and beyond the steady
rain upon that large and hopeless force, making its
last few miles and nearing, as it thought, its end.

As the light broadened a deep mist enveloped
them all around. It was a mist through which

the fine, almost imperceptible rain settled into the already sodden clothes. It mercifully shut out from those discouraged and broken men all sights save their immediate duty. They passed through the streets of a village, the long weary line of them, and more than one of the line took advantage of the fog and of a break in the hustle to hide himself in a side lane in the hope of escaping what was to come. They approached a narrow tumble-down bridge at the head of which, by dint of violence, some sort of order was arranged. The men on foot were thrust back, the cavalry sent forward first, and among the first hundreds Boutroux's troop of hussars, mounted anyhow and wishing they were dead. Even in that fatigue and as he passed it, Boutroux, to whom the things of the eyes were very precious, noticed that the little stream ran milk-white, and he thought it curious.

"Everything," he said to himself, "in this accursed North country is strange!"

A quarter of an hour after, at the head of the rising lane, as the hussars struggled forward, fetlock deep in mud, there loomed through the fog a line of high trees, and it was some slight comfort, after such a march, for the cavalry to find themselves on the great highroad. They were filed off by the left along it, and it was passed along from one man to another that the main camp was close by.

Seven strokes sounded from the cracked old bell of the village below : the sound came harsh and tinny yet muffled through the mist, and when the last stroke sounded the whole mysterious and obscure surroundings were shrouded again in misty silence save for the shuffling of damp feet upon damper earth as the line crawled and tumbled up pell-mell from the brook below on to the height of the road.

Suddenly all their minds and all the imagined landscape beyond the fog was transformed for them by a sound which very few of those huddled thousands had ever heard. It was the sound which all who lived were to hear for twenty years : the unannounced, unbugled boom of guns. Far up to the left along the great highway—upon a height it seemed, from the noise—they were firing. It came and it came again—a mile away perhaps—perhaps more.

Thud! . . . it was the earth that carried the sound. Half a minute's silence, then again— Thud! . . . One could have sworn the dripping leaves upon the high, road-side trees had trembled. The less weary and the younger of the long line of horses stirred at the sound and sniffed the air. . . . Thud! . . . It came again.

What guns and whose had thus opened the game none but the staff could tell—but they were firing, and there was action. For some few moments an alertness and almost a gaiety came into the eyes of these young men, broken with fatigue though they were and with the ceaseless marching of the night.

Boutroux's old horse lifted its head with a faint gesture that years ago might have betrayed a recognition of that sound; but that head drooped again, and the beast stood as weary as ever in the long line of the cavalry drawn up beside the road . . .

A fainter, less certain, a more distant noise began to answer: the enemy had opened his reply. Thud! Thud! . . . the nearer pieces were firing faster and faster, the further batteries opposed followed pace for pace; for an hour it grew from a measured beat to a broken roar, at last a furious cannonade.

But all that business and momentous sound was veiled; and those cannon seemed to be part of ghostly and unseen things.

No shadow of a man approached down the road through the grey murk; only now and then a slight breath of wind, rising as though lifted by the anger of the far artillery, blew a clear space before the eyes of the cavalry. In such a moment could

be seen half a mile of the long road : the infantry
in their ranks waiting ; the wagons drawn up by
the kerb ; a chance group of officers with maps,
watching and straining towards the sound of the
firing. Then the lane, so opened for a moment, as
quickly closed again with new rolls of cloud, and
swallowed up in it the countryside : bare rolling
land ; miserable wet stubble ; the white bare
patches of the famine-fields, where not even rye
could grow. All the while the rumble and the
thunder continued.

A brigade of cavalry passed before them, and
the hussars, dismounted, watched them go by with
envy. They could understand no more of the
welter than their fellows left behind, but at least
they were going to act, and this mere halting in
the rain was one more weight of despair to their
less fortunate fellows.

The clatter of their shoes died away in the fog :
the cannonade had dropped to a fitful exchange of
shots, which at last came only from the further and
more distant guns. The young men were talking
to each other aimlessly ; certain of the infantry, at
the end of the long straggling roadside line, were
too free. They had sauntered up and were speaking with their dismounted comrades of the hussars,
when, as sudden and as unexpected as that first

cannonade, but twenty times more violent, crashing like the fall of some titanic plate of metal, or the clapping to of some vast door, rang another nearer and intolerable firing. It ceased abruptly : two minutes later a novel sound came through the fog ; it was like the noise of flood waters, or of a hurricane in trees at night ; it was the approach of broken men.

First a few, flying in a complete disorder, pierced through out of the fog, stopped, and tried to form again as they came upon the infantry and the cavalry lining the road. Then, as more and yet more poured upon them in the panic, they broke yet again.

So scattered, so pouring by, rallied here and there in confused groups by desperate superiors, whirling in eddies, streaming away in curses and blows and adjurations, half a brigade and more of the stampede fled down the great highway and were swallowed up in the mist again.

The hussars had barely time to note them— one officer was heard saying to another that the wreckage was from Dumouriez's lot—when yet another body came retreating down the great road, in somewhat better plight but heavily mauled.

It was followed by a maimed and jumbled pack

of wagons, with limbers here and there, and here and there the carriage of a broken gun. The horses of the teams had blood upon their flanks, and more than one limber was dragged by a team from which a leader or a wheeler had been cut away, so that the end of the trace hung knotted and severed. Confused and scrambling, that deafening jostle and jolt of wheels went past in its turn : following it, the last of the broken position, and a covering for its flying defenders, walked past with more dignity and in far better order a mounted force. These also passed, and were lost in the mist beyond. The noise of the flight grew less, and ceased altogether. There came up the now empty road two orderlies galloping hard : the officers in command of the waiting roadside line received them. In a quarter of an hour the infantry and the hussars had formed into column and were off eastward again upon their endless business of unexplained advance and fatigue.

The young men had heard cannon, and had seen the beginning of war : they were bewildered, and for the most part they remembered best, of that confused morning hour with its cries of panic and flood of fugitives rolling before them, the *coffee* hot and ample. There had been coffee and bread by the gallon. They all remembered it for many days.

Within a mile they saw through the rising mist, dimly, the spire and the houses of another village upon the great highroad ; behind it a whole field of tents where the main force of Kellermann had waited through that sodden night. But the tents were striking even as they approached, and a vast mass of equipage and train was moving off on to the empty uplands above, while the heads of the columns were being wheeled each in turn off the great road towards the fields above ; the hussars with the rest. The horses dragged as best they could through the morass of those ploughlands, men riding in front picked out the hardest going, and every few moments the whole winding trail of them would halt as the head of it was checked at a soft patch.

The mist shredded and grew thinner ; the wind had risen. The far field line along the sky was plainer, and the soldiers began to tell one another that they were nearing a main position. Far off in the mist, behind them at first, but on their left as the long line of men wheeled northward, sounded fitfully and unseen and muffled the distant guns of the invaders.

The head of the hussars had reached a crest,

the infantry had already occupied its further side, when there came down the irregular mass shouted orders that struck and halted the joints of the column : the two miles of men were to stand.

It was ten o'clock when the halt came. Till noon there was no further movement. The hussars had dismounted again ; the fog rose lighter and lighter yet ; the wind strengthened and scattered it over great patches of dull landscape ; here and there a mass of distant men, the enemy, appeared westward from the height on which the cavalry stood.

Boutroux and his troop were holding their mounts to the leeward of a great windmill which stood up, sheltering them somewhat from the weather ; into the depth of that weather the ill-formed thousands of the army extended, all at haphazard. Beside the mill and along the crest before it were drawn up the foot in every form. Boutroux, from behind his shelter of the mill, saw with a complete indifference battery after battery, six batteries in all, get slowly through the press, and have a way made for them to positions on the ridge of the hill.

All behind the mill and on either side was a confusion of men, chiefly of the mounted forces, scattered pell-mell. On the same sheltered side of the hill lay little packs of men who had fallen out, and the few wounded, and there were groups of sappers as well. Here and there a bunch of the Grenadiers in their tall bearskins ; the mass of cavalry waiting dismounted, and the whole of this reserve without due form or order.

It was noon, and there was nothing forward. Boutroux considered within himself how strange a thing was active service, and how incomprehensible a thing a battle—if indeed this was battle, and battle it surely was, to judge by the perpetual distant cannonade. He guessed vaguely what might be the plan ; abandoned the muddled riddle, and did not even ask his old white horse for aid in such a problem. He crouched there in the lee of the mill, watching the haggard and empty faces of the idle groups about him, wondering what might be doing on the edge of the crest beyond his shelter, watching a barrel of wine slowly dragged up upon two wheels by a donkey, which a most hideous canteen woman of the 98th was leading with difficulty, and blows, through the mud.

All the while the distant guns kept up their ceaseless and repeated booming, and now and then a shell fell wide over the heads of them all, to drop in the further valley and be lost in the mist

of it, and now and then a luckier aim dropped
a solid shot not far from the mill walls, so that
the ground shook with it. Sometimes, much
more rarely, some stroke of even better fortune
for the enemy, or of better aim at a moment when
the wind was steady, would make a dance near by :
a clatter of breakage and a slamming blow, followed
by a scuffle and cries.

But still—there was very little doing. Boutroux
munched his bread, and gazed on the reserves
before him. He saw only a lot of most unfortunate men, drenched as though they had
swum through a pond ; a great welter of horses
also, of wagons, and here and there of provision-
ment ; the smoke of a fire where some one had
lit it for the warming of his coffee in spite of the
weather, and the occasional whistle and thud of
projectiles falling near at hand, set to the irregular,
distant, and sullen boom of the enemy's guns.

Then, as noon turned, the guns of his own forces
took it up—they were not a hundred yards behind
him ; they shook the air, and the ground, and all
his bones. He thought the noise intolerable—it
was just beyond the mill, blasting him to pieces
every quarter of a minute, and drowning all his
senses. But he had to bear it, had Boutroux—
and as for the old white horse, he cared as little

for the nearer as he had cared for the further noise.

The wind was rising, the mist had turned into low clouds that scurried before it. There was now neither mist nor drizzle, though the air was very cold ; the intervals of open sky grew larger and more frequent, and sunlight—for the first time in all those dreadful days—broke upon the tarnished colours of the force. A man strolled up to Boutroux and told him it was worth seeing.

" Worth seeing—what ? " said Boutroux.

" They're beginning to advance," he said. He told Boutroux that from a place a little way back, where there was a gap, one could see everything. But Boutroux didn't want to see : he would stick it out where he was with his horse, in the lee of the mill. The whole thing was quite beyond him.

All the while that damaging and rocking noise of the French guns tormented and bewildered the air. He heard loud shouts of command—the staggering line beyond the mill was suffering some sort of order ; it was massing into three columns. He could see linesmen called up from scattered groups and hurriedly shifting their packs on to their shoulders. He could see men running up to take their places in the tail of companies. Then, during a pause in that incessant firing, he heard a great volley of cheers, and the confused political cries, enthusiastic and young, which reminded him of the street rows at home.

His curiosity got the better of him. He hooked his bridle to the mill door staple, peeped round the corner of the brickwork—and saw nothing. . . . At least only those three great masses of men, all solemnly drawn up together.

They hid from Boutroux the guns that were massed in front, on the edge of the hill, but he did see for one moment Kellermann and his staff mounted and showing high above the line. And as the general rode down the front, just before the sight of him was lost in the press beyond, Boutroux saw him leading and answering the cheers, the three-coloured plume of his hat waved on the point of his sword.

Having so seen, Boutroux went back to his shelter and tried to bear the noise. He was about to soften its terrors by further gentle conversation with his mount, when a crash so very much more abominable than all he had yet heard drove from him the memory of name and place and time. The whole fabric of the mill shivered, the air was a moment stunned and dead . . . the dreadful pause of a second, no more, was followed by a dense cloud of black and pungent smoke blowing

before the high wind past either side of the
building, and in the same moment came up that
terrible unnumbered cry of many wounded men,
shrieking and rising pointed upon a background
of yet more terrible moans. He heard articulate
appeals for death, and next, immediately, he saw
great lumps of the linesmen crouching, turning,
hiding, in every attitude ; a moment later and a
whole brigade was flying past him, with officers
and sergeants cursing in German, striking and
wounding and turning the cattle back with
the sword — it was the German mercenaries
maddened by the explosion of the limbers, and
roaring for safety from such hells. Boutroux
was like a man moored to the pier of a bridge
during the swell of a flood ; he was protected
from that flood of war by the brickwork of the
mill, but he was enclosed with swirls of panic on
every side.

It was soon over. They got the paid men
under control as one gets a fire under control.
The mass was beaten and salved into shape : it
shuffled back into some sort of order again, and
one troop after another of cavalry were got together
and sent forward. The hussars were still left
alone, and empty of business in the shelter of the
hill. No orders came for them. A fatigue came

up (on the crest beyond, the guns still hammered
and banged) ; it came staggering under a great
measure of oats. It was high time, and Boutroux
very contentedly filled his poor beast's nose-bag,
and tied it on. At first the old white horse
would not eat, but Boutroux coaxed :

"I have no wine for you," he said ; "but if you
will eat, like a good beast, I will steal water for
you from the gunners."

The guns went on with their dance more furiously than ever. Now and then an isolated cheer
broke out, recalling to Boutroux that first storm of
cheers when Kellermann had rallied the line two
hours before. Now and then the sharp break of a
shell, the noise and cries of it, or the ground far
before him caught by a chance shot, startled him.
The guns went on. Boutroux was almost grown
part of the deafening on the other side of his mill ;
he had almost forgotten what a day was like in
which there were no guns . . . yet these were the first
guns he had ever known. The thing comes quickly.

Hour after hour throughout the afternoon that
noise occupied the sky, until at last, at about five
(at any rate his stomach, though shaken by the fire,
told him it was the time for soup), the slow
dropping of the cannonade became more and more
marked to the listener.

As the fitful and rarer shots succeeded one
another, the mist, now wholly blown away, the
open sky which had followed it, were in turn
succeeded, perhaps as a sequence to so terrible
a duel, by a black ceiling of storm; the last vengeance of that fortnight's weather poured angrily
upon the thousands massed and huddled round the
mill, passed, and it was clear again. No further
battery fired, save, very far off to the northward,
one stray shot and then another. The cannonade
was done.

Then, for perhaps half an hour, a curious silence
fell. Boutroux, behind the mill, could not but
notice it. It was so silent that the creaking of
the mill sails on their pivot in the slight but
persistent wind occupied his imagination. It was
so silent that the whispered conversation of men as
awed as himself sounded loud, as it would sound
in a room. The scud went slowly and noiselessly
on eastward across the heaven, and so low it seemed
like a reef above them. One shot broke the
silence at last solemnly. The smoke of it rose
from the Mont Yvron, a mile away. It was
fired as a signal is fired. There was no reply.

For yet another half-hour this strange silence
endured. It was suddenly broken by the sharp
clangour of bronze; a bugler too aged for a

soldier, some unlettered peasant of the old time
broken in many wars, was sounding the assembly
not a hundred yards away from the mill.   By
his side a little drummer with the facings of a royal
regiment, very strict and (for such an army!) almost tidy, recalled the traditions of the King and
of less fatiguing days.

The men came flocking up from every side as
to a town crier, for they saw with these two a third
who, from a horse, had an order to read. Boutroux
stood where he was, too careless to move, yet
interested in that sight.

" Horse," said he wisely, " this is a battle. Do
not forget it. Things are not in manhood what
boyhood imagines them ! . . . This has been a battle.
We shall have to boast of it by and by."

The loud high voice of the man who read the
order sounded clear, though too far to be followed
through the rain-washed air ; mounted as he was
he showed against the declining light of that soaked
September evening in a manner prophetic and
wonderful enough.   But Boutroux thought to
himself : " It will be time enough to learn the
news in a moment when he shall have done."   He
had not long to wait. The reading was soon over,
the little drummer drummed a smart and lengthy
roll, the bugle sang out again, and the three or

them went on to another group. The crowd of torn uniforms and broken faces which had gathered to hear the order dispersed, each man to his food and to his place. Those who had been next Boutroux under the mill sauntered back again.

"You have missed something, Sergeant," said one.

"What is that?" said Boutroux.

"It has been a great victory . . . and there's a Republic," said the other.

"What is a Republic?" asked Boutroux.

"I don't know," said the soldier, "but it sounds bloody good!"

So he said, and he swore that he would go and drink to the Republic; and as he so swore he shambled off to where the canteen woman dispensed at an immoderate price small cups of wine from her travelling barrel on wheels.

As for Boutroux, sitting on the wet ground with his back leaning upon the foundation of the mill, he looked up at his horse and murmured,—

"Dear friend, do you hear that? . . . But I forgot: you never answer me. Well, then, I will tell you of my own accord. We have won a great victory . . . and there's a Republic."

For the first time in so many days the old horse, full of oats, at last neighed. He wanted water.

Boutroux slowly lifted himself from his cramped position, not without a twinge in the joints after such weather. He lounged up to a gun near by and collared the pail.

"Orders not to lend that pail," grumbled the man left with the gun.

"Sorry," said Boutroux. He walked off with it, and begged the old white horse to drink the dirty stuff. "It tastes of powder, I know," he said, "but so does all this cursed trade." The old horse drank at last.

Boutroux pushed open the mill door, helped himself to a nice wisp of straw, and very slowly and methodically began to groom his beast, telling it as he did so all manner of entertaining things.

CHAPTER XXII.

*Which shows the Disagreeables attendant upon
the Use of Amateur Drivers in the Conduct
of Artillery; especially when they are
pressed for Time.*

THE September dark had fallen; through the
thick air the stronger stars could just be
palely seen. Away along the Prussian lines a few
smoky fires began to burn, notably in front of a
small inn which lay upon the great Paris road, within which inn the King of Prussia, and Brunswick,
and the princes of the French blood—and, for that
matter, near by, young Goethe the poet—were
assembled. But what did the Army know of such
things?

Those who still cared to look over what had
been the field of that day's cannonade saw nothing
save the vague line which a roll of land makes
darker against the dark sky of a cloudy evening,
and here and there those smoky blotches of dull

12

red light coming and going with the drift of the murk, and marking the line of the allies. A young soldier—a volunteer caught in during the march— came up with a lantern in his hand and peered into the door of the mill; his face was full of joy, for he was still three-quarters civilian, and he had education, and the literary side of the thing appealed to him. He said,—

"A great day, Sergeant."

To which Boutroux replied, with as little brutality as he could manage,—

"I don't suppose that was your message."

"No, Sergeant," said the lad, "but I couldn't help saying it;" and he sighed contentedly.

Boutroux continued to rub down the old horse with a wisp of straw, and as he did so he noted painfully that the beast shivered.

"Sergeant," said the lad, "I've come with orders."

"Well, what are they?" said Boutroux, grooming away, and not looking round.

"We sleep on the ground, Sergeant."

"Naturally," said Boutroux; "and I hope you will not find it too damp. I sleep in the mill. Dismiss."

"Sergeant, they're calling all the sergeants round in the regiment."

"You should have said that at first, you hoofed and horned fool!" answered Boutroux, with the politeness of the service. "I'll be back soon," he said to his horse as he shut the mill door behind him, and followed the boy to where a number of the non-commissioned rank were running up to receive the regimental orders. The subalterns were there, each delivering the message for his troop; and in the darkness, on a mount that still held itself well after all these days, Boutroux saw the figure of his colonel; and as he saw it he remembered vividly those hot hours in the south, and the young officer meeting the Commissioner to the Armies, the sudden promotion, and all the bewildering jumble of the eastward march under this man's growing command. The order was read to them by the light of a lantern; they were told that the operations had been completely successful; the cannonade was made to seem to those young men and old, huddled together, a national and a determining victory. They were told that the invaders were routed.

Meanwhile, a mile away, the invaders lay in occupation of the crest that they had held all day long, and the issue, as men knew better in proportion to their rank, was only a little less doubtful than the day before: a little less doubtful in this, that the great unformed mass of the French levies had just barely stood; they had not been driven and broken into the forest of the hills.

But the soldiers were content to accept the new legend, and for the first time in all those days gaiety ran through the regiment. Even the prospect of a night upon that drenched soil did not disturb them, and Kellermann had wisely seen to it that wine should come up from the village : men were filled with wine before they slept. In the line the companies, in the cavalry the troops, clubbed for the purchase of the liquor ; the canteen made its enormous profits, and for the first time since the beginning of the wars the peasants were doing business too.

To one of these, bringing his barrels in upon an open cart, Boutroux went up and spoke.

"Friend," said he, "will you not sell me some of your wine?"

The man shook his head. He was under orders to sell to no one but to the canteen. "Written orders," he said, "and signed by the colonel upon the paper of the Republic." He spoke that last word with so much dignity that Boutroux looked at him curiously.

"I have heard already that the Republic is crawling on ; but if only you would give me some wine, since you are not allowed to sell it, we might discuss the matter."

"I have no wish to discuss it," said the peasant, "and I certainly will not give you wine. We have been a Republic these twenty-four hours."

"See how stingy Republics are!" said Boutroux. "Why, in the old days such as yesterday and the day before, when there was no Republic, men could have wine for the asking, and sometimes for the taking. It has not mended things, your Republic; but I will go and tell the news to my horse. I do not need your wine. Only tell me something I do not quite understand. What is the name of this place?"

"This place?" said the man clumsily; "it has no name."

"I thought as much," said Boutroux, "by the look of it during the daylight. But I suppose you live somewhere: there is some sort of a village with pigs in it and more mud?"

"Down below," said the man, jerking his thumb, "is my village."

"What do you call it?" said Boutroux.

"Valmy," said the man.

"I must remember that name," said Boutroux. "When one gets out of active service it is a great thing to remember the names of battles. I can see myself sitting in an inn with a great scar upon my face (got from a cart-whip) ; the yokels shall stand me drinks while I tell them the dreadful things I did round and about the mill at Valmy, and what wounds I had, and how bewildered a man is and yet how exalted under fire."

With this he sauntered off; the main force drew off through the darkness, but the hussars held on ; and all night long until the bugles under the dull and misty dawn he slept by his horse in the mill, and with the morning they assembled for the march again.

The line was formed, the regiment was in column and began picking its way through such huddled groups of the soldiery as were left on the height, past broken limbers, here and there the body of a man, cases of food and of powder, scraps of the bread brought up at the end of the day before—all the litter of position which has been held by many thousands.

"I thought as much," murmured Boutroux to himself, as the column very gradually wound its way out of the confusion of men and things and headed eastward down the great empty rolls of chalky land, "I thought as much. They never say it in the history books, but it is what I always imagined to be true. After a great victory one heads away from the enemy. But we must not make too sure, my dear," he continued to the old horse, patting its neck ; "we may be outflanking, or enveloping, or doing some other monstrous thing. Or we may be concentrating ; but it does look uncommonly like a peaceable and well-ordered retreat so far as the Lambs are concerned."

As for the Lambs, they went forward easily enough. There was nothing in the attitude of those spent boys with their sprinkling of veterans, and their young colonel at the head, to suggest any emotion of retreat or of victory. They were still maundering on whithersoever they might be led, which is the whole trade of soldiers. The grooming had been very imperfect, the horses were badly splashed, but after the cannonade the respite had given ample time for provision, and at least the poor beasts had been well fed and had drunk their fill of the white chalky water of the Champagne Pouilleuse.

A few miles off Argonne stood up, a long low wall against the eastern sky, dark with its miles and miles of trees ; and beneath it, at the foot of a gap, a spire and a confusion of little buildings marked Ste Menehould.

They went on thus two hours, parallel bodies beginning to move with the advance of the day ;

they reached the gates of the market-town, and as they reached them Boutroux noticed that his mount was done. Horses, especially the trained horses of cavalry, will so work up to the last moment, and then, without excuse or complaint, their end comes upon them. The old white horse stumbled twice, and Boutroux checked it, pulling it up and cheering it as he had done now for so many days. But the horse did not respond and did not lift its head. It had not many hundred yards to go. His horse so failing filled him with a superstition. He put his hand in his tunic to his chain and his medal. The medal was gone.

Just as they got within the streets of the town Boutroux, with the last troop of the long column of the regiment, heard a clatter and a crashing of wheels coming down the slope of a side street. It was the hired local drivers—peasants bringing in a battery. There was a complete confusion ; the weight of the pieces and of the limbers on the steep incline had been just too much for the wretched teams, and the whole weight of the business was pouring down unchecked on to the high-street. The horses stumbled and slid together, some had already caught in their traces, one or two thrown, and the most of them sliding upon the wet paving.

The troop had barely turned their eyes to notice the danger, when Boutroux, appreciating it more rapidly than any other of his equals, shouted, as men do in accidents, forgetting rank,—

" Lieutenant, wheel them to the right, and bring up alongside the next file ! "

The lieutenant looked round, startled, began to see what was happening, and had the sense to obey the suggestion. He shouted the order, the men urged their mounts, the whole half-hundred were pulling away quickly from the shock of the battery just as its ungoverned impetus came upon the high-street. Boutroux, rounding up at the end, was watching his men to see that they should just escape the peril, when the old white horse could do no more. The attempt at speed which its rider had conveyed to it was the point which determined its end. It stumbled—a pole of the near limbers was within a foot of its flank. Boutroux, forgetting friendship and forgetting ties, pulled at the curb brutally. The poor beast lifted its head and jerked it in an attempt to rise, failed, and fell.

It fell right upon the sergeant's left leg before he had time to drag it from the stirrup ; and as it fell, the pole, the wheels of the limber, and the teams came in a mass over the fallen horse and rider. . . .

Before Boutroux's eyes was a mad confusion of plunging horses, men's feet in the stirrup irons, and the thongs of whips ; Pascal's old head tossing twice in a convulsive movement. But the sight was conditioned and controlled by an intolerable and increasing pain. This vision of pain, noise, and wild movement, all mixed and kneaded together, lasted not a moment. The sergeant was soon alone with pain, and with pain only. The air about him grew dark ; he saw, heard, knew, felt nothing but the pain, nor did anything else remain with him. The pain extended and became a part of his being.

Less conscious than a man in a drunken sleep, he knew that they were moving him, but he knew it only by newer and sharper experiences of pain : he was conscious of that so fully that there was room for nothing else. It was as though the colour upon which his closed eyes dully gazed, the dark red colour which was round him somehow like a cloak, was the very colour of pain. Then, by God's mercy, this awful form of consciousness grew dull ; his spirit and his body ached, but only ached. He had sunk into a sort of use and custom of dull agony, and soon this also passed, and without repose and without refreshment he sank into something deeper than his deepest sleep.

CHAPTER XXIII.

In which the Girondin complains of the Weather.

WHEN consciousness returned to Boutroux, it returned two-fold : he was clear of himself, of his name, of his regiment, he was especially clear of every tiny detail of light and shade and colour at the moment before he fell ; and he was conscious again of pain—of pain now not only mudding all the rest or overspreading it, but of the pain as a separate thing. And the pain had location : it was his thigh and his right groin.

He groaned and opened his eyes. He was in a little bed, the last of twenty or thirty that lay in a line along the wall of a room so lengthy that it seemed almost a corridor. The opposite wall which faced the foot of his bed was a line of gaunt and dirty windows against which the rain still drove and poured ; the distempered walls were splashed and grey, cracked in parts and caught with dust at the corners. At the far end, to which his eyes could just turn (for he could move no part of his body nor lay his head to one side), a large white mark, showing against the duller background of the wall, was the place where a crucifix had hung for many years and had shielded the surface from the effect of the light. He was in one of those hospitals which the forces had hurriedly arranged in the public buildings of Ste Menehould : it was a convent, dissolved these two years ; a day or two before it had been the quarters of some of Dumouriez's men. Their obscenities and their jests were scribbled on the walls, and intermixed with them the name of the regiment which had occupied the building. So much he gathered and no more. He could hear on the paved street without the rattle of passing wheels, and he distinguished the clank of cannon. . . . The occasional cries of command reached him also ; but with these familiar sounds, there were others in that room less familiar and most distressing to the broken man. From four beds away came a continual monotonous groaning as regular as the breathing of sleep, and at the far end of the room a man in attendance was roughly quieting or attempting to quiet some boy whom a wound had driven light-headed, and who broke out time and again into shrieking snatches of marching songs.

As Boutroux so lay, he saw coming up the room at the foot of the bed a doctor attached to the armies, a civilian bearing pinned to his sleeve the badge of his temporary duty. With him was one of the men told off for this fatigue, one of the few men that could be spared for such a duty, himself ill enough, white and miserable, and only spared to walk the hospital because he would have been unable to march.

The doctor came up to the bed; the attendant recited the case, the name, and the regiment, from notes he held in his hand. Boutroux, wondering what they would do with him, lying helpless and gazing at them without much friendship, saw that the doctor was a settled bearded man, a surgeon, perhaps, one of deliberate movements and of fixed manner. He pulled back the bed-clothes and put his hand upon the hip of the sergeant, who gave a loud cry of pain. He pressed his hand, careless of such an effect, and of other cries that followed it, upon the groin and upon the thigh; he passed it up to the lowest of the ribs; he found there that the pain ceased; with a fixed pressure of the fingers that maddened his patient—but his patient could not move—he quickly discovered for himself the main part of the business, and, having done so, he put the bed-clothes back and moved off again.

Boutroux lay alone, staring at the ceiling and suffering beyond all measure at having to lie there unfriended and uncompanioned, with no interest but perpetual pain. He thought : "If something had hit me during that battle of theirs—for I understand it was a battle—they would have put me on the straw and I should have had some one of the regiment by me ; there would have been an open wind upon my face. But here I am in prison, with a sickly linesman to visit me, perhaps every three hours, and a townsman doctor to maul me in silence only to decide whether or no I am to die."

Hour after hour passed and he lay thus, knowing nothing and able to learn nothing. The bed next him was empty, and he had spoken to the form in the bed beyond, but he had got no answer, and that form had lain all these hours unpleasantly still : the face was turned away from him ; he could see but the hair of the head above the clothes. He wondered when some one, any one, would come to exchange a human word with him.

That longing was no longer bearable, he thought, when the attendant reappeared in that long room of suffering and death, and Boutroux called to him. He marvelled to find his voice so thin and bodiless. The man came up and stood over him. The man's paleness, his unshaven chin, a cough into which he fell from time to time, showed how he had been invalided for this service upon the wounded.

"What is it, Sergeant?" he said, and gave a cough again, his thin and narrow chest torn and racked by it. "What is it, Sergeant?"

"Am I to eat?" said Boutroux. He found as he said it that his voice was not only thin, and himself, as it were, without will and bloodless, but that he had to modulate his every tone lest the vibration of the sound, conveyed to his broken tissues, should add to his pain.

The man shook his head. "Not till you take a draught the doctor wrote for you," said he.

"Then give it me," said Boutroux.

"The doctor said that if you were suffering great pain I was to give you the draught. Are you suffering great pain?"

"Yes," whispered Boutroux.

"You are sure?" said the man. "Mind you, I was not to give you the draught unless you were suffering great pain!"

"Oh, I am suffering enough," he sighed;

"give it me. Then afterwards, perhaps, I may eat."

The man went off; he was gone, as it seemed, an intolerable time; he came back with a bottle of thick syrup and a broken cup.

"The doctor did not tell me how much water I should mix it with," he said doubtfully, as though Boutroux could have helped him in such a dilemma.

"Give it me neat," said the sick man; "I have found things do more good that way." And he drank a measure of the sweet, thick, and dark stuff—a thing that in health he could not have done.

The attendant bore off the bottle and the cup, and Boutroux, as he lay—even before that other had reached the door at the further end of the room—felt a change. He still suffered pain: in a way it was the same pain; then his mind grew somewhat freer of it. He suffered it still, but he did notice it less and less, until, in rapid phases, each a better phase than the last, his pain occupied him no more. But something inward began to see matters extremely clear. He was constrained to shut his eyes, so much clearer was that inward sight than the dull walls of the room and the dull windows of it. The colours of what he saw were especially plain : there was a tarred log wall and fern litter, and his white horse old and absurd, the horse Pascal. The horse was splashed and steaming from the weather ; he looked round for something to groom it with : there was not even straw. But as he looked, the door of the place opened and the bright sunlight came dancing in. It shone upon a face and body that seemed to him immortal, and the girl's arms, as she smiled and laughed at him, held a great load of shining straw ; she cast it at his feet and said she had brought it because she knew he needed it, and that she would bring him what he needed, no matter where, and from no matter what far places, for ever, and for ever, and for ever. And he, laughing back at her, said : " Joyeuse ! No one would believe it outside the regiment, but there is nothing like straw and plenty of it for the grooming of a beast."

" Good bright straw," she answered, " from the fields where it ripens in the sun."

He was taking it by a handful to groom his beast, when, even as he groomed it, he found himself walking with it, leading it by the bridle, and he found himself alone. He found himself alone with it, leading it through a woodland way, and he talked to it and asked it a question, saying : "Pascal, have we lost the regiment and the service ? "

And the horse answered him naturally enough : " Yes, Sergeant, we have lost the service, and the service us. And I am glad of it for evermore ! "

He answered : " You are right. It is the service that makes this dullness and this pain."

For as he walked beside the old horse in the woodland way, he felt that the walking hurt him more and more : in the groin . . . dully, then more sharply, the pain increasing upon him : the horse and the woods were part of the pain : everything was a part of it, and everything was growing grey, and the woodland colours about him were fading. They faded into greys and dull reds, through which his eyes, opening slowly, saw again the walls of the room and the long line of windows streaming still with rain. At his side and near his head he distinguished the doctor standing. The doctor was speaking not to him but to the attendant.

" The opiate," he said, " has had but little effect upon him, and that is the sign I feared. Next time, if he needs it, it will have less." He shrugged his shoulders and moved off to the other beds.

Boutroux was broad awake. The light seemed to be the dull light of a wet evening, but he could not be sure whether it was his eyes that failed him or the light outside that was falling. He called in his feeble voice, and the attendant came again.

"What is it, Sergeant?" he asked.

"What is the time?" said Boutroux in the low voice of a man hoarse and tired.

"I will go and see," said the man.

"No, no, don't go and see. I want to speak to a man. . . . Sit down gently upon the bed."

The attendant sat down and looked at him stupidly enough, and not very patiently.

"What did the doctor say?" whispered Boutroux.

The other looked awkward. "He said he couldn't do much good," he answered at last.

"For how long?"

"Oh, it might be any time," replied the other dully.

Over the young sergeant's face there passed for the first time in those hours an expression of pain which was not physical.

"What did they do," he said, and he was whispering with difficulty now, " . . . to the old horse?"

"He was all broken in the leg and side, so they shot him," said the man.

"And am I not so broken?" said Boutroux.

The man had nothing to answer: he got up

to go away. Then he heard, or thought he heard, an odd thing from Boutroux's bed : the words,—

"I should like to see a priest."

The man turned and stared. The sergeant might as well have asked for the stars or for fairy gold. Then he laughed stupidly, as he often did when he heard wounded men raving, and he began moving off again : he could just hear the voice feebler, hoarser, and lower than ever begging him to halt.

"Is it still raining ?" it said.

"Yes," he answered.

"What weather !" sank the voice. And after that it spoke no more.

The attendant waited a moment curiously half-way down the room ; he called out to the bed : "Are you suffering pain ?"

But there was no answer.

THE END.

Established 1798

T. NELSON
AND SONS
PRINTERS AND
PUBLISHERS

NELSON'S
NEW NOVELS

---

*Uniform with this Volume and
same Price.*

ALREADY PUBLISHED.

Second String.   ANTHONY HOPE.

This brilliant social comedy contains all the qualities which have
given Anthony Hope his unique reputation as a historian of modern
life. He introduces us to the society of the little country town of
Meriton, the tradespeople, the loungers in the inn parlour, the
neighbouring farmers and squires, and especially to Harry Belfield,
the mirror of fashion in the county and candidate for its represen-
tation in Parliament. We see also his former school friend, Andy
Hayes, who has returned from lumbering in Canada to make a
living at home. The *motif* of the tale is the unconscious com-
petition of the two friends, of whom Andy is very willing to play
"second fiddle," did not character and brains force him to the
front. The young squire of Halton is too selfish and capricious to
succeed, and in spite of his loyalty to friendship, Andy finds himself
driven to take his place both in love and in politics. A host of
characters cross the stage, and the scene flits between Meriton and
London. The book is so light in touch, so shrewd in its obser-
vation, so robust and yet so kindly in its humour, that it must be
accorded the highest rank among Anthony Hope's works—which
is to say, the first place among modern social comedies.

III

Fortune. J. C. Snaith.

Mr. J. C. Snaith is already known to fame by his historical novels, his admirable cricketing story, his essay in Meredithan subtlety "Brooke of Covenden," and his most successful Victorian comedy "Araminta." In his new novel he breaks ground which has never before been touched by an English novelist. He follows no less a leader than Cervantes. His hero, Sir Richard Pendragon, is Sir John Falstaff grown athletic and courageous, with his imagination fired by much adventure in far countries and some converse with the knight of La Mancha. The doings of this monstrous Englishman are narrated by a young and scandalized Spanish squire, full of all the pedantry of chivalry. Sir Richard is a new type in literature—the Rabelaisian Paladin, whose foes flee not only from his sword but from his Gargantuan laughter. In Mr. Snaith's romance there are many delightful characters—a Spanish lady who dictates to armies, a French prince of the blood who has forsaken his birthright for the highroad. But all are dominated by the immense Sir Richard, who rights wrongs like an unruly Providence, and then rides away.

The History of Mr. Polly. H. G. Wells.

If the true aim of romance is to find beauty and laughter and heroism in odd places, then Mr. Wells is a great romantic. His heroes are not knights and adventurers, not even members of the quasi-romantic professions, but the ordinary small tradesmen, whom the world has hitherto neglected. The hero of the new book, Mr. Alfred Polly, is of the same school, but he is nearer Hoopdriver than Kipps. He is in the last resort the master of his fate, and squares himself defiantly against the Destinies. Unlike the others, he has a literary sense, and has a strange fantastic culture of his own. Mr. Wells has never written anything more human or more truly humorous than the adventures of Mr. Polly as haberdasher's apprentice, haberdasher, incendiary, and tramp. Mr. Polly discovers the great truth that, however black things may be, there is always a way out for a man if he is bold enough to take it, even though that way leads through fire and revolution. The last part of the book, where the hero discovers his courage, is a kind of saga. We leave him in the end at peace with his own soul, wondering dimly about the hereafter, having proved his manhood, and found his niche in life.

Daisy's Aunt.
E. F. Benson.

It is Mr. Benson's chief merit that, without losing the lightness of
touch which makes good comedy, he keeps a firm hold upon the
graver matters which make good fiction. The present book is a
tale of conspiracy—the plot of a beautiful woman to save her young
niece from a man whom she regards as a blackguard. None of
Mr. Benson's women are more attractive than these two, who fight
for long at cross-purposes, and end as all honest natures must, with
a truer understanding.

The Other Side.
H. A. Vachell.

In this remarkable book Mr. Vachell leaves the beaten highway
of romance, and grapples with the deepest problems of human
personality and the unseen. It is a story of a musical genius, in
whose soul worldliness conquers spirituality. When he is at the
height of his apparent success, there comes an accident, and for
a little soul and body seem to separate. On his return to ordinary
life he sees the world with other eyes, but his clearness of vision
has come too late to save his art. He pays for his earlier folly in
artistic impotence. The book is a profound moral allegory, and
none the less a brilliant romance.

Sir George's Objection.
Mrs. W. K. Clifford.

Mrs. Clifford raises the old problem of heredity, and gives it a very
modern and scientific answer. It is the story of a woman who,
after her husband's disgrace and death, settles with her only
daughter upon the shore of one of the Italian lakes. The girl
grows up in ignorance of her family history, but when the inevitable
young man appears complications begin. As it happens, Sir George,
the father of the lover, holds the old-fashioned cast-iron doctrine
of heredity, and the story shows the conflict between his pedantry
and the compulsion of fact. It is a book full of serious interest for
all readers, and gives us in addition a charming love story.

Prester John.
John Buchan.

This is a story which, in opposition to all accepted canons of
romance, possesses no kind of heroine. There is no woman from
beginning to end in the book, unless we include a little Kaffir
serving-girl. The hero is a Scottish lad, who goes as assistant to

a store in the far north of the Transvaal. By a series of accidents he discovers a plot for a great Kaffir rising, and by a combination of luck and courage manages to frustrate it. From beginning to end it is a book of stark adventure. The leader of the rising is a black missionary, who believes himself the incarnation of the mediæval Abyssinian emperor Prester John. By means of a perverted Christianity, and the possession of the ruby collar which for centuries has been the Kaffir fetish, he organizes the natives of Southern Africa into a great army. But a revolution depends upon small things, and by frustrating the leader in these small things, the young storekeeper wins his way to fame and fortune. It is a book for all who are young enough in heart to enjoy a record of straight-forward adventure.

Lost Endeavour. JOHN MASEFIELD.

Mr. Masefield has already won high reputation as poet and dramatist, and his novel "Captain Margaret" showed him to be a romancer of a higher order. "Lost Endeavour" is a story of adventure in Virginia and the Spanish Main. A Kentish boy is trepanned and carried off to sea, and finds his fill of adventure among Indians and buccaneers. The central episode of the book is a quest for the sacred Aztec temple. The swift drama of the narrative, and the poetry and imagination of the style, make the book in the highest sense literature. It should appeal not only to all lovers of good writing, but to all who care for the record of stirring deeds.

Panther's Cub. AGNES and EGERTON CASTLE.

This is the story of a world-famed *prima donna*, whose only daughter has been brought up in a very different world from that in which her mother lives. When the child grows to womanhood she joins her mother, and the problem of the book is the conflict of the two temperaments—the one sophisticated and undisciplined, and the other simple and sincere. The scenes are laid in Vienna and London, amid all types of society—smart, artistic, and diplomatic. Against the Bohemian background the authors have worked out a very beautiful love story of a young diplomatist and the singer's daughter. The book is full of brilliant character-sketches and dramatic moments.

Lady Good-for-Nothing. "Q."

Sir Oliver Vyell, a descendant of Oliver Cromwell, is the British Collector of Customs at the port of Boston, in the days before the American Revolution. While there he runs his head against New England Puritanism, rescues a poor girl who has been put in the stocks for Sabbath-breaking, carries her off, and has her educated. The story deals with the development of Ruth Josselin from a half-starved castaway to a beautiful and subtle woman. Sir Oliver falls in love with his ward, and she becomes my Lady and the mistress of a great house; but to the New Englanders she remains a Sabbath-breaker and "Lady Good-for-Nothing." The scene moves to Lisbon, whither Sir Oliver goes on Government service, and there is a wonderful picture of the famous earthquake. The book is a story of an act of folly, and its heavy penalties, and also the record of the growth of two characters—one from atheism to reverence, and the other from a bitter revolt against the world to a wiser philosophy. The tale is original in scheme and setting, and the atmosphere and thought of another age are brilliantly reproduced.

No better historical romance has been written in our times.

The Simpkins Plot. GEORGE A. BIRMINGHAM.

The story tells how a red-haired curate discovers in a harmless lady novelist, seeking quiet for her work, a murderess whose trial had been a *cause célèbre*. He forms a scheme of marrying the lady to the local bore, in the hope that she may end his career. Once started on the wrong tack, he works out his evidence with convincing logic, and ties up the whole neighbourhood in the toils of his misconception. The book is full of the wittiest dialogue and the most farcical situations. It will be as certain to please all lovers of Irish humour as the immortal "Experiences of an Irish R. M."

Sampson Rideout, Quaker. UNA L. SILBERRAD.

Miss Silberrad's work has of recent years grown rapidly in reputation, and her new novel is one of the best historical romances of the day. It is the story of the love of a Quaker manufacturer for a great lady. The scene is laid in the Wiltshire downs, in Stuart times, and the atmosphere of the age and place is reproduced with extraordinary fidelity and charm. The book is primarily a study of a man and a woman both exceptionally endowed in mind and character, who, starting from the opposite sides of life, meet on the ground of a common goodness.

Adventure. JACK LONDON.

This novel is the fruit of Mr. Jack London's recent experiences in the South Seas—experiences more full of wonder and peril than any romance. It is the story of a young English planter on a lonely island, and an American girl who appears suddenly from nowhere and becomes his business partner. The book does not belie its name : adventure is of the very essence of the lives of this man and woman, and the love story which crowns the tale is no less adventurous and original than the rest. Mr. London writes of strange places with the vividness and realism of one who himself has dared and seen most things.

THOMAS NELSON AND SONS,
London, Edinburgh, Dublin, and New York.

THE
NELSON LIBRARY
OF COPYRIGHT FICTION.

Price Sevenpence net.

FORTHCOMING VOLUMES.

THE GOOD COMRADE.   Una L. Silberrad.

In this charming story Miss Silberrad breaks fresh
ground. It is a tale of the bulb-growers of Holland
and of English provincial life. It is, above all, the
study of a heroic woman, done with all Miss Silberrad's
subtlety and truth.   (*April* 19.)

MULTITUDE AND SOLITUDE. John Masefield.

It is the story of a man of letters who is disappointed
with his craft and yearns for some more active career.
He finds it in a campaign against sleeping sickness in
Africa. The grimness and realism of the African chap-
ters have not been surpassed in modern literature.
"Multitude and Solitude" is a type of the new romance,
which is at once philosophical and dramatic. (*May* 3.)

THE GIFT.   S. Macnaughtan.

(Author of " The Fortune of Christina M'Nab.")

In this story, as in "Selah Harrison," Miss Macnaughtan
gives us a study in religious temperament. In "The
Gift," however, she is concerned with the development
of a woman's soul. The delicacy and subtlety of the
treatment is as remarkable as the touches of delightful
comedy which no work by Miss Macnaughtan can
ever lack.   (*May* 17.)

THE DOLLY DIALOGUES. Anthony Hope.

This is the book which, when first published, made Mr. Anthony Hope's reputation as a writer of social comedies. Dolly, Lady Mickleham, is the first of the witty and irresponsible ladies who for the last decade have enlivened English fiction. She is also by far the best, and the gravest reader is captivated by the grace and humour of the Dialogues.

WHEN VALMOND CAME TO PONTIAC.
Sir Gilbert Parker.

In this charming story Sir Gilbert Parker tells of the fortunes of a young adventurer in Canada in the early nineteenth century who claimed to be the son of the great Napoleon. The mystery of his life and his tragic death make up one of the most original and moving of recent romances. The author does for Quebec what in other works he has done for the Western and Northern wilds—he interprets to the world its essential romance.

THE GENTLEMAN FROM INDIANA.
Booth Tarkington.

In this book the author of "Monsieur Beaucaire" tells a story of his own country. "The Gentleman from Indiana" is a tale of a young university graduate who becomes a newspaper owner and editor in a Western town, and wages war against "graft" and corruption. His crusade brings him into relations with the girl who had captured his heart at college, and their love story is subtly interwoven with his political campaign. It is one of the best of modern American novels, and readers will delight not only in the stirring drama of the plot, but in the fresh and sympathetic pictures given of the young townships of the West.

THE NELSON LIBRARY.

Price Sevenpence net.

CONDENSED LIST.

Arranged alphabetically under Authors' Names.

T. NELSON & SONS, London, Edinburgh, Dublin, and New York.